For Every Radio Requirement—

First published 2012 by Loddon Valley Press, 16 Kibblewhite Crescent, Twyford, Reading, Berkshire, RG10 9AX, UK
ISBN 978-0-9570773-0-0

British Library Cataloging-in-Publication Data.
A catalogue record for this book is available from the British Library.

Design by Aleph Studio, Greenwich, London.

Printed and bound by Hastings Printing Company Limited, St Leonards on Sea, East Sussex, TN38 9BJ.

A Radiophone in Every Home.

William Stephenson and the General Radio Company Limited, 1922-1928

Ian L. Sanders and Lorne Clark

General Radio *

**Trade Mark Registered,
18th December, 1923.**
(Permission Army Council)

This work is dedicated to the memory
of Gordon Bussey, F.R.Hist.S. (1936-2011).

Broadcasting has created a vast new field for recreation and education.

Available to all, are elaborate programmes in music, classical and popular, the most virile and valued of the gems of literature and oratory, the drama unfolded in championship sporting events, announcements and lectures of vast economic import – a wide and diverse field requisitioning the masters of interpretation to deliver in person their messages in music and speech.

A revolutionary change has been effected by the advent of wireless; one that has been accepted in manner that is perhaps too matter of fact. For even the broadest mentality may well be stunned with the realisation that the isolation of culture is no more, that into the humble home, into the isolated community, radio has entered, bringing with it the great messages of words and music that for ages have been confined to a fortunate few.

A Famous Name. Since long before the days of Broadcasting, the Trade Mark, "General Radio", on a wireless installation or component, has been accepted as a guarantee of quality; quality of material and quality of workmanship – proof of efficiency, proof of advanced design.

W. Stephenson

Continuing the high-technology tradition – the General Radio Company premises at 235, Regent Street, London, W.1; home of Apple Inc.'s flagship London retail store in 2011.

The Importance of Integrity

This is a period of transition for the radio industry. The first flush of easy success has faded ; the process of stabilization has begun. It will witness the passing of not a few makes, and as a consequence thereof, an unprofitable experience for the Trader who handles them.

Every Dealer might well take stock of the situation to-day ; look forward two, five or ten years, and wisely select his line with chief consideration for the integrity and permanence of the manufacturer.

Our products are always "better"; our manufacturing facilities unexcelled ; our advertising and selling co-operation genuinely helpful.

Further, the soundness of those standards to which we have adhered since long before the days of broadcasting, is demonstrated by the increased demand for our apparatus. It is a significant fact that most leading Dealers are pushing General Radio Sets and parts with profit and satisfaction. The General Radio Dealer policy provides the fullest measure of merchandising and advertising co-operation.

General Radio

The Wireless Trader, February 1924.

Contents

General Radio *

wants a first
class Agent
(Distributor)
to handle
sales for the
whole of

SCOTLAND

Only ex-
perienced
representa-
tives, with
good con-
nections and
capable of
carrying
reasonable
stock, will be
considered.

——— *Sales Department* ———

**GENERAL RADIO
COMPANY LIMITED,**
Radio House, 235 Regent Street,
LONDON - - - W.1.

* "General Radio" on a
Broadcast Receiver or
Component means that it
is definitely guaranteed to
give absolute satisfaction.

Wireless Trader, March 25, 1925.

Foreword

As someone who has been involved all his life in vintage radio collecting, and who for the past 35 years has been a writer and researcher on the subject, I am very excited about this new book by Messrs. Sanders and Clark. Where others tread the safe path of focussing on the giants of the radio industry (worthy as they are), here the authors stride out and champion one of the small firms who came and went in just a handful of years at the dawn of the industry in the 1920s, yet left an unexpected and surprisingly rich legacy for radio collectors and historians to get their teeth into today.

What started out as an idea for a short article about the General Radio Company Ltd. has blossomed into a wide-ranging and valuable book on its rise and fall. Unearthing and tracking down the story, and the personalities associated with GRC, must have been a great challenge, but obviously an enjoyable one which the authors enthusiastically share with the reader. If the writing is easy on the eye, so too are the wealth of wonderful illustrations and photographs of the actual radio sets, horn loudspeakers, headphones and pieces of original ephemera, so beautifully laid out in the book by Christine Bone of Aleph Studio.

I am sure that *A Radiophone In Every Home* will prove a wonderful success, and maybe will inspire others to research similar lesser known vintage radio companies in the future.

Happy reading!

Jonathan Hill, Author and Photographer, Exeter, November 2011.

Preface

This work evolved from an idea that the authors had for a short article on the General Radio Company Ltd. However, as the research developed, it became clear that there was a far bigger story to be told. From the colourful characters involved in the Company's founding to the many peripheral businesses and associations of the Company itself, the story continued to develop in diverse and unexpected directions, as though it had taken on a life of its own.

The aim has been to produce a book that will appeal to both the non-technical reader and those with a more specialised interest in the history of early radio and television. Striking this balance has not been easy, but we hope that we have succeeded in achieving the goal to some degree at least. Taming this beast, for that is what it seemed to be at times, has been most challenging. Many people have generously given their help and support along the way, for which the authors are truly grateful.

Whilst we cannot claim to have covered every aspect of the Company's history and products, we have attempted to provide as broad a picture as possible, given the available sources. Some aspects, such as details of the Company's earliest products, have remained elusive – perhaps more facts will come to light in time. The authors would be pleased to hear of any relevant information and may be contacted via either of the email addresses given below

This book then is the chronicle of a company long gone, but with a fascinating story all its own. We trust that you will enjoy it.

Please note that there is no known connection between General Radio Company Limited of Great Britain and the General Radio Company of the United States – the latter was better known as *GenRad* in later years. Not surprisingly, there is sometimes confusion in the literature between the two entities.

Ian Sanders and Lorne Clark
September 2011

Contact details for the authors are as follows:
Ian Sanders: author@crystal-sets.com
Lorne Clark: lorne@earlywireless.com

Acknowledgements

The authors wish to thank Martyn Bennett, Carl Glover, Jonathan Hill, David Read, and Chris Simmonds for their valuable support and encouragement throughout this work. Martin Francis, Erwin Macho and Robert Murray generously provided photographs of General Radio Company receivers and Gianfranco Rocchini kindly allowed the reproduction of a photograph of a Cox-Cavendish medical instrument. John Wakely drew our attention to a British Thomson Houston receiver manufactured by Cox-Cavendish and provided photographs of the same. Thanks are due to David Rudram of the Amberley Museum and Heritage Centre of West Sussex and to Mike Kemp for the generous loan of items in their collections. The authors would also like to thank Jonathan Hill for generously allowing us to reproduce the image on page 69 and for providing the Foreword.

The assistance of Lisa Whitehead of Morphy-Richards Limited in providing a photograph of company founder Donal Morphy is much appreciated. A special mention must also be made of Catherine Campbell of Information Services, Canada Science and Technology Museum Corporation, Ottawa, Ontario who was particularly helpful with the research into the activities of General Radio Company of Canada. Gordon Bussey, F.R. Hist.S., kindly provided the authors with copies of period literature from his private collection, scans of these being prepared by Robert Mance. Just before he died, Gordon had kindly offered to proof read the manuscript for this book. Sadly this was not to be.

Access to the General Radio Company's files held at the National Archives, Kew and to the extensive journal collections held at the British Library, Colindale is also most gratefully acknowledged, as is access to the Churchill Archives, Cambridge. Finally, the authors would also like to thank Charlotte Connelly, Assistant Curator of Computing and Communication, The Science Museum, London, for arranging access to the museum's reserve collection stores. Many of the original photographs are by Carl Glover.

A Comment on Pricing

Decimal currency was introduced to Britain in 1971. Prices quoted in this book are in the pre-decimal sterling currency units of pounds, shillings and pence (£ s. d.) that was in use at the time the General Radio Company was in operation. Under the old sterling system, one pound was divided into twenty shillings and one shilling divided into twelve pence. Thus there were 240 pennies to the pound, so that a post-decimalisation *new penny* is equivalent to 2.4 *old pennies*. One shilling was the equivalent of five new pence.

For amounts less than one pound, the conventional notation was to use a forward slash symbol to separate shillings and pence, as shown in the following examples:

Three shillings 3/-
Five shillings and three pence 5/3d
Seven shillings and six pence .. .. .. 7/6d and so on.

For amounts of one pound or more, the full notation of pounds, shillings and pence was generally used:

Two pounds, six shillings .. .. .. £2 6s. 0d.
Five pounds, fifteen shillings and six pence .. .. .. £5 15s. 6d.

Occasionally, the use of a monetary unit known as the 'guinea' was applied to the pricing of more expensive receivers. One guinea was equivalent to twenty-one shillings (£1 1s. 0d.). Pricing in guineas was frequently used in the past to add prestige to 'big-ticket' items such as furniture, motor cars and professional fees. Although last minted in 1813, the guinea, with its nominal value of £1.05, is used today by auction houses and, in the equestrian world, prizes for major horse races are still quoted in guineas.

When correlating the buying power of a pound sterling in the 1920s with its equivalent buying power in 2011, the authors have used the following excellent resource:

http://www.measuringworth.com/ppoweruk/

A Comment on Patents

In this book patent numbers are shown as a 2-letter country code followed by the numerical patent reference number, e.g. GB123456 refers to British patent no. 123456.

The following 2-letter country codes are used throughout the text:

CA - Canada
FR - France
GB - Great Britain
US - United States of America

The Wireless Trader, January 21, 1925
and February 4, 1925.

A Radiophone in Every Home.

William Stephenson and the General Radio Company Limited, 1922-1928

A bronze statue stands in the grounds of the Legislative Building in Sir William Stephenson's birthplace of Winnipeg, Manitoba, Canada. Sculpted by artist Leo Mol, the statue depicts the future Managing Director of General Radio Company in his First World War aviator's uniform. Following his Intelligence work on behalf of the Allies in the Second World War, Stephenson played a key role in the establishment of what would become America's Central Intelligence Agency. A replica of the statue was presented to the CIA as a gift by the Intrepid Society of Winnipeg, Canada in 2000.

Statue of Sir William Stephenson in WWI flying suit, Legislative Building grounds, Winnipeg, Manitoba.

Introduction

Regular broadcasting in the UK started late in 1922, with the formation of the British Broadcasting Company. During the first few years, some two thousand radio manufacturers sprang up to seize the business opportunities that this new medium promised. Some were small sole trader affairs operating out of garden sheds and garages, while others were large limited companies with extensive facilities and prestigious addresses.

Prospects for these companies appeared promising for a while, but the vast majority were destined to fail within a very short time, many through chronic lack of investment. However, it was by no means only the smaller enterprises that went to the wall. Even the larger, well-funded enterprises were not immune from failure.

In spite of its relatively short six-year lifespan, General Radio Company Limited was certainly not 'typical'. Neither were its directors, who counted amongst their number an entrepreneur turned spy, (later codenamed Intrepid), an individual responsible for introducing to the world a sticky, brown, savoury spread (Marmite) and a young engineer who later became the undisputed master of home appliances in the twentieth century. Of these, the indisputable driving force behind the company was the enigmatic Canadian, Sir William Stephenson* of Intrepid fame. The chronicle of the company that he founded before achieving fame in other fields is very much his own.

Entering the wireless business in the early 1920s, at the very start of broadcasting in Great Britain, General Radio Company produced an extensive array of receivers, accessories and wireless components. By any manufacturer's standards the range was impressive, spanning crystal receivers priced at just £1 18s. 0d. to a substantial six-valve cabinet receiver retailing at a staggering £169 15s. 0d. The company trademark – the mustachioed general, sporting monocle, medal ribbons, riding crop and spurs – added a touch of solid, albeit a little old fashioned, early twentieth century Britishness to the whole enterprise. All-in-all, the company image epitomized the post-war patriotic zeal of the time.

A noteworthy feature of General Radio's marketing strategy was the imaginative and constantly changing array of advertisements published in the myriad of technical magazines that flooded the market during the first years of national broadcasting. For this reason some emphasis has been placed on reproducing a selection of the material here.

In view of what appears to have been a most successful start, it is all the more surprising that General Radio Company should, within just a few years, have met the same fate as literally hundreds of other wireless firms unable to compete in the new business. It is also surprising that examples of their products have survived in such small numbers. General Radio was certainly no small-scale amateur enterprise and its receivers were of high quality by the standards of the day. Further, the company went out of its way to incorporate a host of innovative features into its products. But such was the turmoil in these pioneering days of domestic radio that anything was possible. Perhaps the very scale of the company's extensive support organisation was just too much for the period. Traumatic, no doubt, for the engineers and business entrepreneurs involved at the time, it is now the stuff that makes up the fascinating history of the countless companies, large and small, that perished in the early years of British broadcasting.

* Much confusion surrounds the details of the life of Sir William Stephenson, including his birth date and schooling and his First and Second World War exploits. Whether this has occurred deliberately or not is a matter of some conjecture. In producing this work, the authors have tried to sort fact from fiction and give as accurate an account as possible of the founder of General Radio Company.

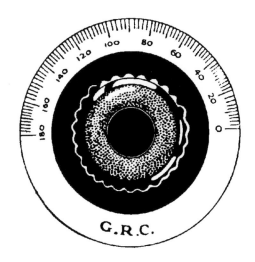

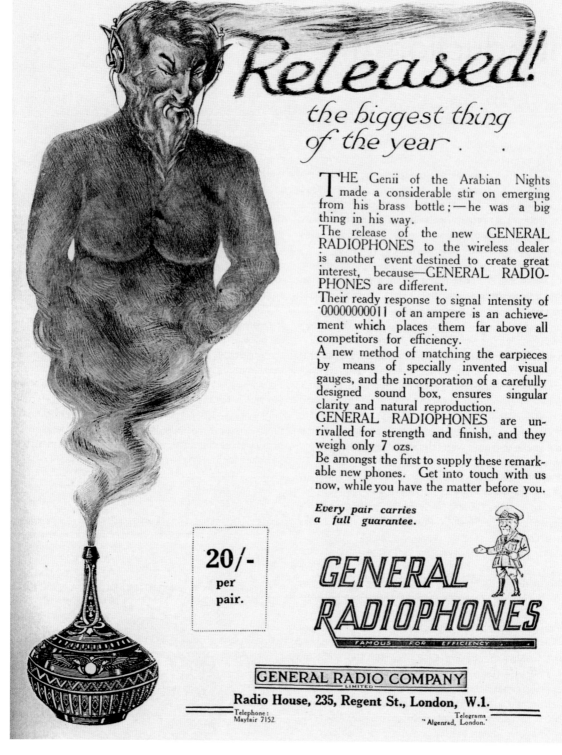

The Wireless Trader, May 1924.

Company Origins

Broadcasting has gone through its trial stages and survived. The Radiophone has become institutional, won for itself a definite place in the home, and risen from the stature of a scientific toy to the proportions of a great force for good in both the fields of recreation and education. Amazing technical progress has linked arms with the genius that has guided the steady improvement in scope and quality of the programmes of the air.

General Radio Company Brochure, 1923.

General Radio Company Limited (the company expressly avoided the use of 'The' in formal documents) was registered on June 26, 1923 with a nominal capital of £30,000, divided into 30,000 individual shares of one pound each. The new Limited Company was built on the acquisition of an existing sole trader business known as General Radio Company, owned by William Samuel Stephenson and based in Maida Vale, London. Stephenson, a Canadian born in Winnipeg, emigrated to the UK shortly after the First World War. During the war he had distinguished himself as a pilot in the Royal Flying Corps and it was in this Service that he had his first exposure to the science of radio communication[1]. In 1920, drawn by the prospect of a public broadcasting service, similar to the pioneering station in his home of Winnipeg which was financed by a government issued license, Stephenson purchased an interest in two companies[1,2,3] – General Radio Company referred to previously (as sole trader) and the Cox-Cavendish Electrical Company Limited, a leading manufacturer of X-ray and electro-medical apparatus.

Stephenson, who achieved considerable fame in later life as a member of the Secret Service during the Second World War, had been introduced to the business potential of manufacturing domestic wireless apparatus by his friend William Gladstone Murray, a fellow Canadian flyer known to him from the war years[4]. Murray, in his early 30s, was at that time publicity manager for the Radio Communication Company, whose managing director, Major Basil Binyon, was one of the founding directors of the British Broadcasting Company. It was partly on Binyon's recommendation that, in 1924, Murray was taken on by the BBC's head, John Reith, to be the fledgling company's first Director of Public Relations[5]. Murray, by all accounts a colourful and outgoing personality, later clashed with Reith and the BBC establishment and was eventually forced to resign in 1936. In the early years of General

Radio Company Murray must have provided a very useful personal link between Stephenson and the hierarchy of the British Broadcasting Company, particularly during the General Strike when General Radio Company distributed the text of BBC broadcasts.

It is not clear exactly when the name General Radio Company first came into use. The earliest advertisement using the name seems to have appeared in July 1922 when the then sole trader business was operating out of premises at 105, Great Portland Street, London. The company name first appears in the London telephone directory in October 1922, with the same Great Portland Street address.

By March 1923 Stephenson was running his wireless enterprise, now as a shareholder member of the British Broadcasting Company, from a factory operated by Cox-Cavendish at Twyford Abbey Works, Acton Lane, Harlesden, North London. During 1922 and 1923, Cox-Cavendish's medical business was not generating a profit and, in anticipation of the business opportunities presented by the start of broadcasting, the company embarked on the development of its own wireless receivers and headphones. In fact, in the fifteen months ending June 30, 1923, Cox-Cavendish invested some £5,600 (about a quarter of a million pounds in today's terms) in the development of wireless apparatus. It appears, however, that Cox-Cavendish never actually produced receivers under their own name. In the Director's Report for June 30, 1923, it was revealed that the company had, in the last twelve months, entered into *"a very satisfactory agreement with a leading firm supplying wireless telephony instruments"* to manufacture wireless apparatus on a contract basis. The same Director's Report also announced the appointment of William Stephenson as a company director. Although not named, the *'leading firm'* was almost certainly the British Thomson-Houston Company of Rugby. A surviving example of a BTH portable receiver of 1922 carries a label showing that it was built by the Cox-Cavendish Electrical Company.

Enjoying early success, Stephenson was already employing a substantial workforce even before the limited company was formally registered. According to one biographer at least, confusingly named William Stevenson, General Radio was, in 1923, *"marketing thousands of small home receiving sets for BBC listeners in the British Isles"* [1].

In the General Radio Company's Articles of Association of June 1923, Stephenson – then living at 86, Lauderdale Mansions, Maida Vale, London, N.W.6 and describing his occupation as 'Radio Engineer' – was joined by three other subscribers, each taking one share in the newly formed General Radio Company:

Frederick Wissler of Heath House, Shooter's Hill Road, Blackheath, a British subject of Swiss origin. Wissler, a natural entrepreneur, had recognized the commercial potential in the discovery in 1886 by the German scientist, Justus Liebig, that a protein-rich food could be produced from yeast waste from the brewing industry. In 1902 Wissler, with his German partner George Huth, was co-founder of the ubiquitous Marmite Food Products Company. In the early 1920s, Wissler – in addition to his primary role as Managing Director of Marmite Food Products – was a director and vice-chairman of the Cox-Cavendish Electrical Company. Thus his association with General Radio was a result of the collaboration between the two companies, put in place after William Stephenson's purchase of interests in both enterprises.

Arthur Morphy, a shipbroker of Moorsfort, East Sheen, Surrey. In 1923, Arthur Morphy, O.B.E. was the chairman of Cox-Cavendish Electrical Company prior to its association with General Radio Company. Morphy, born in Greece, was apparently something of a shipping entrepreneur before arriving in Britain. Cox-Cavendish documents dated September 1922 show Arthur Morphy living in Patras, Greece with his occupation described simply as a 'ship-owner'.

Brian Harold Morphy, a 'Wireless Engineer' of 36, Lancaster Gate, West London. Brian Morphy had earlier been a director of Harry Cox & Company at the time of its merger with the Cavendish Electrical Company in September 1919. It was the amalgamation of these two companies that led to the formation of the Cox-Cavendish Electrical Company. After the merger, Brian Morphy assumed a director role with the new company and held that position at the time of Stephenson's appointment to the board of Cox-Cavendish.

Two other Directors, C.M. Farquhar and E.W. Willis, were apparently appointed in 1923[6]. Whilst the Articles of Association record Willis occupying the position of Company Secretary, no mention is made of Farquhar. It is possible that Farquhar was connected with General Radio's short-lived Canadian company.

On July 27, 1923 General Radio Company's 'Allotment of Shares' shows that Stephenson was the major shareholder taking 11,000 shares, followed by Wissler (5,000 shares), Arthur Morphy (4,000 shares) and Brian Morphy (1,000 shares). Although not specifically stated in the General Radio documents, according to the Cox-Cavendish Director's Report of December 1923, Stephenson had taken the title of Managing Director on purchasing a controlling interest. Playing both a business and a technical rôle, however, he continued to be referred in the technical press as the company's 'Chief Engineer'.

On February 28, 1924, a change in address of the registered office of the Company to the highly desirable location of 235, Regent Street, Oxford Circus, London, W.1. was filed by Brian Morphy, now Company Secretary. At some point the Company also opened a showroom at 105, Regent Street. Documents for May 1924 reveal that Stephenson had now taken up residence at the Regent Palace Hotel and, more importantly, recorded the death of the director Frederick Wissler. In January 1925 his sons, William Edward Stanley Wissler and Clement Leslie Wissler, as executors of their father's estate, assumed ownership of their late father's shares. The documents also reveal that William Wissler was 'Director of Marmite'. By June 1925 all of the Wissler family shares had passed to William.

The final change to the company's board occurred in January 1926 when Arthur Morphy's son, Donal William Morphy then of 26, Church Road, Richmond, became a director of General Radio. Morphy, born in Greece, went on to co-found the celebrated home-appliance manufacturing giant Morphy-Richards, in partnership with his colleague Charles Richards. Specialising in the production of electrical and gas household appliances, Morphy-Richards was soon to become an international household name.

In addition to his talent as an entrepreneur, Stephenson was an innovative engineer. A key patent relating to an improvement in the design of headphone earpieces, specifically addressing the construction and factory adjustment of the diaphragm assembly, was granted in 1925[7]. Branded *General Radiophones*, the company's headphones figured prominently in their advertisements and were a key component of their product line. Indeed, during much of 1925 and 1926 headphones were the only product to be advertised in trade and amateur journals. In addition to those carrying the General Radio name, Stephenson also produced headphones for Canadian Brandes Limited for a short period during the early 1920s.

William Stephenson – Inventor, Entrepreneur, Spy...

Mr. Stephenson is a confirmed optimist... In his work we find a happy blend of Canadian "Go-aheadiness", British thoroughness, and a cheerful faith in the future of British enterprise and methods – all of which have left their mark on an undoubtedly successful business.

The Wireless Trader, March 11th, 1925.

Sir William Stephenson was born in Winnipeg, Manitoba in January 1897* as William Samuel Clouston Stanger to William Hunter Stanger from the Orkney Islands and his Icelandic wife, Sarah. Following the death of his father in November 1901, Stanger's widow, unable to support her three children, gave up the four-year old William to be raised by her friend Kristin Stephenson and her husband, Vigfus, a labourer at a Winnipeg lumber yard. The young boy took the name Stephenson, after his Icelandic foster parents. By all accounts Stephenson was a quiet, studious child and what today might be termed a loner.

After completing six grades of elementary education, Stephenson left school, aged about twelve or thirteen, and started work at the Sprague lumber yard. Later he worked as a telegram delivery boy for the Great North West Telegraph Company eventually becoming an operator responsible for the sending of telegrams. He was an employee of Great North West Telegraph when World War I broke out. In January 1916, he volunteered for service in the Winnipeg Light Infantry – his enlistment papers give his occupation as telegrapher.

Stephenson departed for England, arriving in July and was attached to the Canadian Engineer Training Depot. After a brief training period he was sent to France, but was gassed soon after arrival and returned to England to recover. His technical aptitude enabled him to achieve the rank of sergeant and in April 1917 he was accepted into the Royal Flying Corps. By February 1918 he was flying Sopwith Camel fighters at the front. He received a field commission as a lieutenant and shortly afterwards was promoted to captain. After scoring a number of victories against enemy aircraft, he was awarded both the Military Cross and the Distinguished Flying Cross at the age of just 21 years. In July 1918, however, he was shot down east of Saponay, Frère-En-Tardenois, most likely by Ltn. J. Grassman of Ja10. However, there are rumours that it was actually a French observer that mistakenly fired at him.

Arriving back in St. John, New Brunswick in 1919, Stephenson returned to Winnipeg. Here he demonstrated the first indications of entrepreneurial talent by teaming up with friend Charles Russell to form the Franco-British Supply Company in order to manufacture the *'Kleen Kut'* tin-opener. The opener, a two-handled device developed in Germany[2,5], had allegedly been 'liberated' from a store room at the prison camp where Stephenson was being held. The German originator of the tin-opener, prevented from patenting the device outside Germany by the outbreak of war, unwittingly gave Stephenson his first business opportunity. In addition to the manufacture of the tin-opener, the company acted as agents for stainless steel cutlery, automobile accessories and various other hardware.

Vigfus and Kristin Stephenson, 1912.

* Stephenson's birth certificate gives January 23, 1897 as his date of birth, while the 1901 census shows January 16, 1897. Stephenson's year of birth is sometimes given as 1896. On his enlistment papers for the 101st Oversees Battalion of the Canadian Expeditionary Force, dated January 12th, 1916 he incorrectly gave a birthdate of 11th January, 1896. At the time, therefore, he was still just 18 years old (albeit only a matter of days away from his 19th birthday). Whether or not the discrepancy in the date was to facilitate enlistment is a matter of speculation. In any event, the error was never corrected later in life – at least his marriage certificate would suggest this.

Birthdate – Conflicting Documentation

There is much confusion over William Stephenson's actual birthdate. This extract from the 1901 Canadian census (above) gives the date as January 16, 1897 (under his birth name of Stanger). This conflicts with the date of January 23, 1897 shown on the certified copy of his birth certificate.

The confusion is further compounded by Stephenson's Attestation Paper (right) in which he gave his birth date as January 11, 1896. The Attestation Paper, itself dated January 12, 1916, records Stephenson's enlistiment for the 101st Overseas Battalion of the Canadian Overseas Expeditionary Force. At that time he was still just 18 years old so it is possible that he gave an earlier birth date to improve his chances of acceptance into the services.

A new company, Stephenson-Russell Limited, was incorporated in February 1921. It is unclear where Stephenson obtained the capital for this venture. One source says that it was financed with support from his foster father. However this seems unlikely, given Vigfus's occupation as labourer. Questions about the sources of Stephenson's capital during his formative years are endemic. Expanding on previous activities, the partners intended to sell stock and deal in patents and trademarks. It was during 1921 and 1922, in connection with the business ventures of Stephenson-Russell Limited that William Stephenson seems to have made contact with some of North America's pioneer radio companies such as Radio Technology Laboratories of Newark, New Jersey and Haynes Radio of New York. This would likely have been his introduction to the commercial opportunities in the emerging wireless field, although as a pilot during the war he would undoubtedly have had first-hand experience with radio communications. In any event, Stephenson-Russell Limited failed within eighteen months and the company filed for bankruptcy in August 1922. According to one biographer[3], Stephenson became 'a difficult person to find' following the collapse of his company.

Some accounts state that Stephenson lectured at the University of Manitoba after the war – but there is no authenticated record of this. His formal education seems to have ended with elementary school, making a university position unlikely.

Following his company's bankruptcy, Stephenson returned to England in 1922. This was possibly at the request of Admiral Reginald "Blinker" Hall, to assist in the start up of a team of cryptanalysts. "Blinker" Hall, who acquired his nickname through an unfortunate twitch in one eye, had been impressed by the strategic importance of Stephenson's reports on enemy aviation tactics during the war.

Stephenson was certainly also attracted back to England by the business potential that existed in the United Kingdom for the development and manufacture of wireless apparatus. Working with fellow wartime pilot Gladstone Murray and the Canadian newspaper

First World War ace – above: the young Captain Stephenson; below left: Stephenson (right) and comrades, Beauvois, 1919; below right: Will Stephenson (right) and comrade Baldwin, c1919.

CAPT LUSSIER . CAPT PIDCOCK . LT STEPHENSON.
BEAUVOIS. MAY 1918.

Stephenson in London, 1924, at the time he was Managing Director of General Radio Company.
William Stephenson and Mary Simmons were married in South Kensington, London on July 22, 1924.

magnate Lord Beaverbrook[1], he made the case for a public broadcasting service. He believed that the characteristic reserve of the British public in response to plans for national broadcasting had held back wireless development, certainly compared to the situation existing in North America.

By the early 1920s, Stephenson had invested his remaining capital (or possibly borrowed capital, given his bankruptcy) in an existing London-based wireless enterprise operating under the name of General Radio. His original concept was to develop and market a comprehensive range of wireless sets at a reasonable price, and so to open up the latent British wireless market. In spite of this, the company is known to have produced some very expensive luxury receivers.

It was, however, through the development of a picture transmission system, not domestic wireless receivers, that Stephenson reportedly became wealthy. His technology for the transmission of photographs by wireless was adopted by the world's newspaper industry in the mid-1920s and apparently generated substantial income for the inventor through royalties[2].

Undated photograph of William Stephenson with his six-valve cabinet receiver of 1922. This equipment is often mistakenly described in the literature as his 'Seeing by Wireless' apparatus.

Stephenson's fortunes also took another turn when he married the American, Mary Simmons, in July 1924. Mary French Simmons was the daughter of a wealthy tobacco grower from Springfield, Tennessee and Stephenson had met her on his ocean crossing from Canada to Britain. Their marriage certificate shows his occupation as Managing Director of General Radio Company, but his age is incorrectly given as 28 years, likely based on his Service records. Also, both Stephenson and his new wife are shown as living at 2, Hanover Terrace, London W.2. although there is no other record of them ever having lived at this address. In another anomaly, his (foster) father is recorded with the Anglicised name *William* rather than the actual Nordic *Vigfus*. Such discrepancies in the records have become a part of the enigmatic life of Sir William Stephenson, often to the frustration of historians and biographers. It is interesting that his father was shown as being 'of independent means'. This is surprising, given his father's earlier occupation of labourer, but may simply have been Stephenson adding a touch of 'spin' to his background.

In October 1928, Stephenson became a director of the newly formed Symphony Gramophone and Radio Company Limited. The new company had purchased the assets of the respected, but recently dissolved, wireless firm A.J. Stevens, including the manufacturing facilities in Wolverhampton. Symphony produced mains and battery-powered radiograms, a portable wireless receiver and cabinet loudspeakers. The company, however, was in existence for less than eighteen months. One product, the battery-powered radiogram, had reliability problems associated with the thin circuit board. The subsequent customer returns resulted in the company's early demise in March 1930.

In the early 1930s, Stephenson spent some time working on the emerging technology of radar with Robert Watson Watt. Later, Stephenson reportedly experimented extensively with coded signalling techniques (having obtained a German *Enigma* system in the 1920s[2]). This together with his extensive and influential circle of contacts started him on the surprising road to becoming an Intelligence expert.

Great War air ace – Service Records.

Demise of Stephenson-Russell Company

It was through the dealings of the Stephenson-Russell Company that William Stephenson was first exposed to the potential of the domestic wireless business. Although the Canadian company was short-lived, and despite its unfortunate demise, the experience did not deter Stephenson from going on to pursue the business in his mother country.

The Stephenson-Russell Company filed for bankruptcy in Winnipeg on August 13th, 1922. The company's bankruptcy records indicate that only Wilf Russell received any compensation on cessation of the business operations. Stephenson received nothing and according to the son of one of his adoptive father's friends, Stephenson "lost his shirt" as a result of the business failure. It also seems that the demise was precipitated, at least in part, by a mysterious fire that occurred when Wilf Russell was away and Stephenson himself was in charge. The final payments to creditors were not paid out until August 1924. Of about one hundred companies and individuals who were owed money, only eleven were ever paid in full, the others receiving four and a half percent of the debt[3].

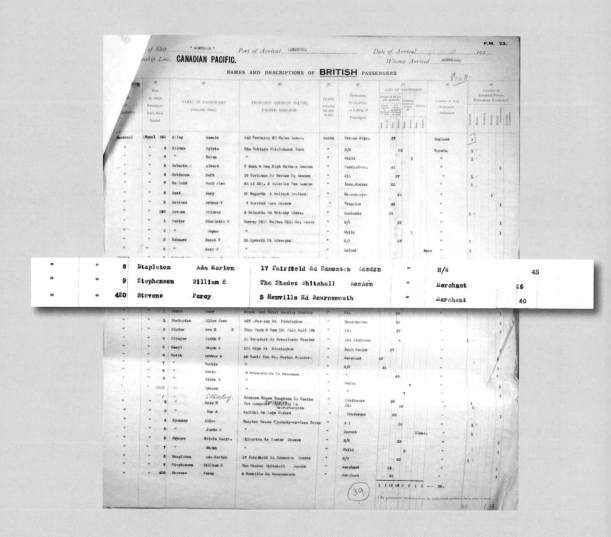

Stephenson's whereabouts following the bankruptcy are not well documented. A manifest of the Canadian Pacific ship *Montcalm* shows Stephenson on board, arriving in Liverpool on May 14 1922. He declared his destination as The Shades, Whitehall, but most likely he was referring to The Old Shades, a hotel in Whitehall. His ultimate residence was recorded as being within a British Protectorate so he was clearly keeping his options open at this stage! Shortly thereafter he became Managing Director of General Radio Company...

The Times, October 5, 1928

*"It's unexplainable. I have him bankrupt
on Victor Street* and months later,
he's being hailed as a great inventor
by the London Daily Mail. For a while
I thought I was researching two entirely
different people."*

Stephenson's biographer, Bill MacDonald
* Stephenson's address in Winnipeg before emigrating to the UK.
Quoted in The Greatest Manitobans, Winnipeg Free Press, 2008.

In the event, William Stephenson – aviator, business-man, scientist and inventor – was to leave his mark on history, not as a developer of wireless receivers, but as an authority on Intelligence. During the Second World War he collaborated with the American Office of Strategic Services (OSS) on behalf of the British Secret Service and eventually became the senior British Intelligence Officer for the western hemisphere with complete responsibility for counter espionage[1,2,3,4].

While Stephenson was still in his early 40s, Prime Minister Winston Churchill appointed him to the influential position of Director of British Security Coordination. At one point Stephenson was effectively controlling much of the British Intelligence infrastructure including MI-5. Operating under the codename Intrepid, his exploits have frequently been cited as the inspiration for Ian Fleming's legendary super spy, James Bond, whose codename '007' may well have been further inspired by Stephenson's WWI service number 700758. A close associate of both Winston Churchill and Franklin Roosevelt, Stephenson is credited with playing an influential role in the creation of the CIA in the United States. In recognition of his wartime services, King George VI conferred a knighthood on Stephenson in the January 1945 New Year's Honours List. Churchill, in recommending him for the knighthood, wrote: *"This one is dear to my heart"*.

Retiring first to New York, he later moved to Bermuda where, like several other prominent Canadians of the time, he spent the rest of his life. Stephenson maintained an active interest in business matters including the launch of a cement manufacturing company – Caribbean Cement Company Limited. He kept in close contact with influential business and political figures and actively promoted international trade. As chairman of the Manitoba Economic Advisory Board he was able to preserve ties to his homeland and was benefactor of a substantial scholarship at the University of Winnipeg.

Sir William Stephenson died in Paget, Bermuda at the age of 93.

Footnote:
While much has been written over the years about Stephenson's life, it has naturally focused on his legendary wartime years in Intelligence. Most works spare only a few lines describing his early involvement with General Radio Company. None mention the company's financial failure after just a few years in operation, while one claims that Stephenson made his *first fortune selling cheap radio sets*[2]. That he made any return on his investment in wireless is unlikely given the early failure of the company.

Donal Morphy

Donal Morphy did not join the board of General Radio Company until January 1926. The Morphy family, however, had been involved with the company since its registration in 1923 with Donal's father, Arthur Morphy and Brian Harold Morphy as original directors. After the winding up of General Radio Company, Donal Morphy worked as an engineer for an electric fire company. Here he met up with Charles Richards, a salesman, and together they formed the private company Morphy-Richards. Their first product, put on the market in 1936, was a 2kW electric fire for home use. This was soon to be followed by a very successful temperature-controlled electric iron. Then came electric toasters, refrigerators and just about every electrical appliance imaginable. The rest is history.

Donal Morphy and Charles Richards at a Morphy-Richards function. By this time, General Radio Company must have been a distant memory for the successful Morphy.

Frederick Wissler

Frederick Wissler's association with General Radio Company was short-lived. Wissler, who co-founded the Marmite Company with George Huth in 1902, died on April 8, 1924, aged 69, having served only nine months as a director of General Radio Company. Prior to his involvement with General Radio, Wissler had been a director of Cox-Cavendish Electrical Company and was likely a close associate of William Stephenson after the latter's purchase into both companies.

A Swiss national, naturalised in 1906, Wissler's estate amounted to some £79,856 14s. 9d. at the time of his death (equivalent to about four million pounds in 2010 terms). His trustees, however, could never have received any return on his investment in General Radio Company. His shares passed to his eldest son William Edward Wissler, who assumed the Directorship of his father's Marmite empire. Little is known of the formative years of the younger Wissler. An entry in the London Gazette for March 1917 announcing his promotion to 2nd Lieutenant, however, reveals he was attached to the Army Service Corps during the Great War.

Unlike radio receivers, Marmite looked much the same in the 1920s as it does today!

William Ewart Gladstone Murray

William Ewart Gladstone Murray (named for the eminent, four-time Liberal Prime Minister at the time of his birth) was born In Vancouver, British Columbia, Canada, on April 8, 1892. An energetic Canadian Rhodes scholar and former Royal Flying Corps pilot, he joined the BBC as Publicity Director from the Radio Communication Company (RCC) in 1924. He was recommended to the post by Basil Binyon – his previous boss at RCC – and developed a large number of influential friends both in journalism and in the House of Commons. Murray was responsible for introducing his wartime friend, William Stephenson, to the commercial promise of wireless receiver manufacture and sales.

After graduating from McGill University in Montreal he worked for a year as a journalist in North and South America; he then went as a Rhodes scholar to New College, Oxford. Between 1914 and 1918 Murray served in the Royal Flying Corps where he flew alongside William Stephenson. Wounded several times, he was awarded the DFC, MC, and Croix de Guerre and was also decorated by the Italian government. After the war, he spent two years as the Aeronautical Correspondent of the Daily Express. A natural publicity man, he subsequently worked briefly as publicity director for the League of Nations Union and as publicity manager of the Radio Communication Company.

Murray remained at the BBC for eleven years. He was Acting Controller of Programmes for three months in 1934/35, where he came into serious conflict with the then Controller of Administration, Admiral Carpendale. Later in 1935, following a major reorganization, Murray became one of two assistant controllers in the programme division. He was particularly popular with his subordinates but was viewed as a threat by BBC Director-General, John Reith. In true BBC-style, Murray was forced to resign in 1936. Murray died in 1970 in Toronto, Ontario, Canada.

Royal Aero Club Record

General Radio Company of Canada

As well as his involvement in the production and distribution of headphones in association with Canadian Brandes, Stephenson maintained a broader contact with the wireless industry in his native Canada. His intimate knowledge of the state of Canadian broadcasting and the growing demand for receivers in that country should have placed General Radio in a good position, relative to other British manufacturers, to penetrate the emerging Canadian market.

In December 1922, General Radio crystal receivers were offered by Eaton's Department Store in Stephenson's home town of Winnipeg, Manitoba. One hundred 'English Radio Sets' were in stock and offered at a special price of eleven dollars each just in time for Christmas. Stephenson also distributed apparatus through other Winnipeg dealers – in March 1923 the Salton Radio Engineering Company announced their quitting of the retail wireless business and offered General Radio products at clearance prices. Eaton's continued to advertise General Radio components such as transformers, condensers and loudspeakers throughout 1924 and 1925, although they seem not to have carried wireless receivers beyond the initial batch offered in 1922. Another well known establishment, the Hudson's Bay Company, also stocked components up until 1926.

General Radio Company staged a substantial demonstration of receivers and accessories at the Canadian National Exhibition held in Toronto at the end of August 1923. It is possible that the X-ray equipment produced by the Cox-Cavendish Company was exhibited in addition to wireless apparatus[3]. The Company's exhibit, under the management of one Stanley Price, was displayed in the Pure Food Building (an indication of the fledgling nature of the wireless industry at that time), under the auspices of Federated British Industries. Held at Exhibition City, a park of some 300 acres in the heart of Toronto and with eighty permanent buildings and hundreds of temporary ones, the exhibition was a grand affair. Intended to display Canada's products to the world it attracted well over a million visitors. Stephenson used the opportunity to announce the formation of a new company – General Radio of Canada.

Mr. Stanley Price was also charged with publicising the new company which was set up to handle the products of the London firm. According to reports of the exhibition, General Radio's presence attracted a good deal of attention, while a rather condescending report in the Canadian journal Radio* for September 1923 declared that the "the demonstration brought the fact home that the British made instruments were equal to anything produced on this continent." To be fair, though, the unconventional General Radio horn-speaker, unusually mounted on top of a rectangular polished mahogany cabinet, was praised as having a particularly clear, distortion-free tone.

Temporary offices were initially established at 70, Lombard Street, Toronto in September 1923. An advertisement placed by the company in the October 1923 issue of Radio offered agencies to interested parties across the country. The response to that request cannot be judged with any accuracy, but indications are that it met with only limited success. Understandably, wireless factors in Canada would probably have been more comfortable supplying North American made products to their customers. In this regard, there is no evidence to suggest that Stephenson produced any products designed specifically for the Canadian market.

By November 1923 a dedicated showroom, The Radio Salon, had been opened by General Radio of Canada at 41, Adelaide Street East, Toronto. A Radio Week opening event was held at the end of the month with a comprehensive range of the company's latest offerings on display. In 1924, Stephenson personally attended the Canadian National Exhibition in Toronto where the company once again exhibited its range of products.

Entries appearing in the Pitman's Radio Year Book[6] for 1923 and 1924 indicate that the General Radio Company was operating an office in Montreal as well as Toronto, although no address was given for either. By 1925, however, only the UK locations were being shown.

Very few sets exported to Canada seem to have survived and the little published material found suggests that the Canadian enterprise never really got off the ground. The winding up of the Canadian company must have occurred within about two years, since no mention of the organisation is to be found in the Canadian Trade Index for 1926. It can only be surmised that General Radio Company of Canada was not all that Stephenson had hoped it would be.

* There were independent wireless magazines called Radio in both Canada and the USA. The references made here are to the Canadian journal.

Canadian National Exhibition, Toronto - 1923

A new company, General Radio Company of Canada, was set up in Toronto in late 1923 to coincide with the Canadian National Exhibition held in Toronto in August/September of that year . The exhibition provided demonstrations of wireless technology by relaying programmes to loudspeakers inside the halls, and was reportedly responsible for a surge of interest in the new medium outstripping the supply from the existing manufacturers[8].

Among the products on the General Radio Company stand were a two valve receiver, with matching two valve amplifier coupled to their cabinet mounted loudspeaker. The company's frame aerial, crystal sets and headphones were also displayed.

Canadian National Exhibition, Toronto - 1923

Cupolas, minarets, spires, domes, striking facades and contours lend an aspect very inviting and pleasing to the eye. They look what they are, vast show cases for the display of a nation's products garnered from factory and farm, mine and forest, lake and ocean, studio and office.

...For a true and complete impression of Canada, her resources, her capabilities and her people, a visit to the Canadian National Exhibition is recommended. No other enterprise of a permanent character yet devised anywhere has met so many wholesome tastes and interests of the general public or has been a more complete expression of the spirit of progress in its particular country.

Exhibition Brochure 1923.

The General Radio Company stand at the Canadian National Exhibition, Toronto.

Popular Wireless Weekly, November 3, 1923.

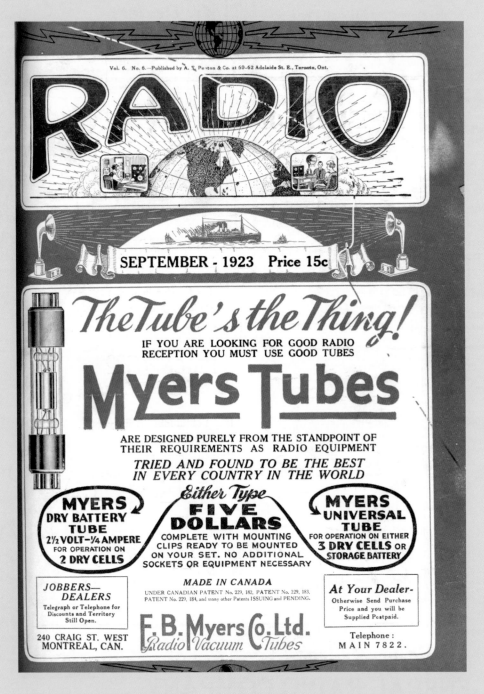

General Radio Company advertised in the Canadian journal *Radio* throughout 1923. The original advertisements solicited customers to contact the UK works for a catalogue. Later advertisements show the establishment of General Radio Company of Canada in Toronto. Temporary offices were initially located at 70, Lombard Street, Toronto. In October 1923 permanent offices at 41, Adelaide Street were set up.

We have developed additional Parts and
Units of RADIO Equipment which are
now in production in our factory.

G. R. C. Radio
Sets & Supplies

ARE OF HIGHEST QUALITY

Write to-day for our Illustrated Catalogue
giving full particulars of our G. R. C. 11
Long Range Tuner, G. R. C. 12 Detector-
Capacity Unit, G. R. C. 13 and 14 Audio
and Radio Frequency Amplifiers.

General Radio Company,
Affiliated with
THE COX-CAVENDISH ELECTRICAL CO., LTD.
Twyford Abbey Works, Acton, Harlesden, London, N.W. 10

Radio, January 1923.

Mr. Dealer:

I am offering the
exclusive selling
agencies, throughout
Canada, for Towns
and Cities not al-
ready covered, write
to-day for my pro-
position.

"General Radio"

We stock complete
Sets and Parts, send
for our catalog—
*"A Radiophone in
every Home"*

GENERAL RADIO COMPANY
——————OF CANADA——————
LOMBARD BUILDING - TORONTO
Distributors for— GENERAL RADIO CO., London, England

Radio, October 1923.

ANNOUNCING

That the opening of my
Radio Salon will be held
Radio Week, Nov. 25th to
Dec. 1st.

———

Call and see us for
Demonstration.

GENERAL RADIO COMPANY
————LIMITED————
41 ADELAIDE STREET EAST   -   -   TORONTO
Write for Descriptive Booklet "A Radiophone in Every Home."

Radio, October 1923.

Mechanical Television and Seeing by Wireless

In 1923 John Logie Baird embarked on the development of a practical television system, but he was not alone. Although Baird's name is the one most closely associated with the invention of mechanical television, many others, including Alan Archibald Campbell-Swinton in the UK, Boris Rosing in Russia and Philo Farnsworth in the United States, invested time and money with the similar aim, but using electronic means. All sought to develop a means of transmitting live moving images to a remote receiver. Whilst historical works on the subject acknowledge the efforts of these and other individuals, they are singularly quiet about the accomplishments of William Samuel Stephenson and his associate at this time, George William Walton.

In 1923 George Walton, as General Manager of General Radio, was working with William Stephenson on developing techniques for the wireless transmission of still and moving images. On April 18, 1923 they applied for a patent 'Improvements for Transmitting Electrically Scenes or Representations to a Distance' which was subsequently granted on July 17, 1924 as British patent GB218766.

The patent described an image scanning technique that utilised twin rotating, slotted discs and, even at this early date, encompassed techniques for both monochrome and colour transmissions.

It incorporated concepts from a previous patent, applied for in December 1922 and granted in March 1924, GB213654 'Keeping Two Rotating Bodies Spaced a Distance Apart in Synchronism'. This earlier patent not only specified a method for keeping the transmitter and receiver scanning motors in step, but also addressed the important problem of wirelessly transmitting the synchronizing tone and the picture information and then separating these components at the receiver.

Stephenson was also reported to have perfected an alternative to the selenium cell as a means of converting light into electrical currents. Apparently, the new device exhibited a much faster response to changes in light level than was possible with the selenium cells in use at that time. Stephenson's improved sensing device was most probably a novel, light-sensitive vacuum cell based on the design described in British patent GB190218 granted to the

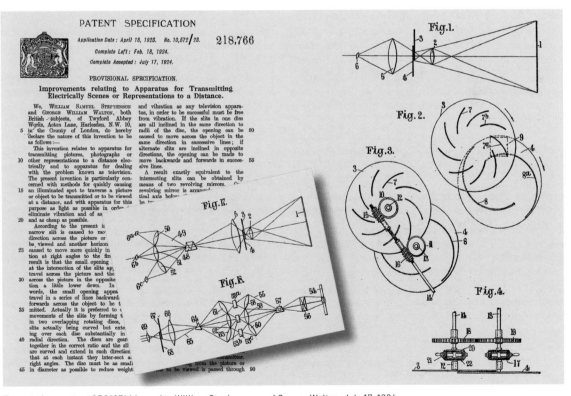

Extracts from patent GB218766 issued to William Stephenson and George Walton, July 17, 1924.

British Thomson-Houston Company (BTH) in 1922.

It is very likely that Stephenson would have had access to such a device through the contract manufacturing relationship that existed between the Cox-Cavendish Electrical Company and BTH.

Announcements in *The Radio Times* and *Popular Wireless and Wireless Review* in September and October 1924, respectively, invited the public to an exhibition at the General Radio Company's premises in Regent Street that apparently included television equipment. Held between September 24th and October 8th, the event was timed to coincide almost exactly with *The National Wireless and Radio Exhibition* organized by the National Association of Radio Manufacturers at the nearby Royal Albert Hall. Open until 10:00pm each evening, the General Radio event was no doubt designed to attract visitors from the trade show. According to at least one source[9], Stephenson came close to beating John Logie Baird in demonstrating the first mechanical television system. Certainly, Stephenson's patent dealing with the synchronising of receiving and transmitting apparatus - a key difficulty in early mechanical systems - dates from about a year before Baird's British patent GB236978 addressing a very similar system for synchronisation.

An in-depth article describing Walton and Stephenson's concepts for television transmission appeared in the US technical journal, *Radio News*, dated April 6, 1925. A detailed description of their system can be found in Appendix IV of this book.

Other than the cited patents, Walton's article in *Radio News* and the exhibition at the General Radio Company premises, little is recorded regarding General Radio Company's involvement in the development of a functional television system. All the evidence (or rather lack thereof) would suggest that neither Stephenson nor General Radio Company went on to seriously pursue the technology to any commercial ends.

As well as his involvement in the transmission of moving pictures by wireless, Stephenson had been active in developing a practical technique to transmit still pictures by wireless. Working with T. Thorne Baker [10,11], inventor of the 'Telectograph', and sponsored by the *Daily Mail* (at that time the newspaper claiming the largest circulation in the world), Stephenson set about adapting the system for wireless transmission and reducing the scanning and transmission times.

Up until this time, the scanning process had been relatively slow. To improve efficiency, Stephenson may well have replaced the existing electro-mechanical scanning system with an optical system, perhaps employing his improved light cell. However, much of the speed improvement may have been due to the introduction of the technique specified in Stephenson and Walton's synchronism patent (GB213654) discussed above.

Their system would have replaced the existing

Headline from *Winnipeg Free Press*, September, 1924

cumbersome and time consuming method in which slowly swinging pendulums were used to synchronise the discontinuous rotation of the image drums. In addition, the same patent described a method of transmitting the image wirelessly. These improvements significantly decreased the time it took to transmit a still image, from some forty-five minutes to just three minutes. The application of such a system would have enabled virtually any existing image transmission apparatus to be adapted for wireless transmission, potentially earning Stephenson considerable royalties.

Images sent by the new method of wireless photography, using Stephenson's improvements, were first published by the *Daily Mail* on December 27, 1922. Hailed by the newspaper as a "*brilliant scientist*", Stephenson found that his technique was rapidly adopted by major newspapers throughout the world. The business became so profitable for its inventor that he reportedly became a millionaire at just thirty years of age[12]. In view of his public success, it is all the more curious that T. Thorne Baker, in his 1926 book *Wireless Pictures and Television*, makes absolutely no mention at all of William Stephenson, George Walton or of any collaborative work.

Stephenson seems to have kept his '*Seeing by Wireless*' enterprise quite separate from the business of General Radio Company. A report in *The Wireless Trader* for March 1923 mentions that the General Radio Company's stand at the *Daily Mail Ideal Home Exhibition*, Olympia in London included an enlarged photograph of H.R.H. the Prince of Wales, transmitted by wireless using "*a new process developed by Capt. Stephenson.*" Stephenson, ever the diplomat, would have no doubt given the photograph due prominence.

After severing ties with General Radio in the late 1920s, George Walton subsequently took out other television related patents. These were to form the basis of a new television company, Scophony Limited, formed in the early 1930s and financed by the entrepreneur Solomon Sagall[13]. The Scophony technology was based on a sophisticated mechanical system in which an image could be projected onto a large screen by means of mirrors mounted on highspeed rotating drums.

Like earlier attempts to develop a mechanical system of television, the Scophony technology was eventually to be superseded by the advances in all-electronic systems using the cathode ray tube.

"Seeing by Wireless"

In early 1922, William Stephenson collaborated with T. Thorne Baker in the development of a practical system of transmitting still pictures by wireless. Baker, a photographic research chemist, had been working on the problems of sending images by wire for many years in association with the *Daily Mirror* newspaper. It was the newspaper's proprietor, Lord Northcliffe, aware of Stephenson's rare combination of technical and entrepreneurial skills, who arranged for Baker to join General Radio Company to develop the technology. For some time Northcliffe had been interested in the potential of wireless photography through his other high-circulation newspaper, the London *Daily Mail*. It is not clear how long Thorne Baker's association with General Radio lasted, but it is likely to have been quite brief. A few years later, in a 1926 publication, Thorne Baker makes no reference to any collaborative venture and in fact mentions nothing of Stephenson's work at all.

PHOTOGRAPHS BY WIRELESS.

GREAT SCIENTIFIC ACHIEVEMENT.

AFTER FIFTY YEARS OF EXPERIMENTS.

"DAILY MAIL" RESEARCH.

Image of two skiers transmitted by wireless appearing in *The Daily Mail*, December 27, 1922, under the banner headline of a *Great Scientific Achievement*.

The accepted method of transmitting pictures electrically was to break the image down into a pattern of dots or lines using a half-tone screen. A corresponding array of *insulating* dots or lines was then applied to a thin, conductive metal sheet wrapped around a rotating cylinder. A stylus in contact with the cylinder scanned the image making intermittent electrical contact with the metal sheet on which the image was printed. The resulting electrical impulses were then sent to a remote receiver. At the receiver a strip of standard photographic film was attached to another rotating drum. For the system to function correctly, it was critical that the drums at the transmitter and receiver be synchronised.

Many methods of achieving synchronism had been proposed with varying degrees of success. The method developed by William Stephenson and George Walton at General Radio was described in patent GB213654 filed as early as December 1922 and issued in March 1924. The technique involved taking a pair of taps from the armature winding of the motor driving the transmitter drum. The taps were taken to a pair of slip-rings which generated a low-frequency alternating tone as the motor rotated. The tone was sent to the synchronous motor at the receiver, either by wire or wirelessly, maintaining synchronism between transmitter and receiver. For wireless transmission, the synchronising tone was used to amplitude modulate a carrier wave on which the intermittent signal from the scanning stylus was superimposed. Filters at the receiver separated the synchronising tone from the image signal, the latter driving a non-polarised relay controlling the light source.

The method of synchronising was revolutionary and appears to be identical to the system proposed by Baird as part of his later patent GB236978 filed over a year later and not granted until July 1925. Stephenson's first wirelessly transmitted picture, an image of two skiers, was published in the December 27th 1922 edition of the *Daily Mail*. The improvements implemented by Stephenson resulted in his *Seeing by Wireless* being used by major newspapers all around the world, making the young inventor a millionaire.

Mechanical Scanning Television

Both Mr. W.G. Walton and Mr. W.S. Stephenson of General Radio Company, London have done a great deal of research work in the matter of the transmission of pictures by radio, and have made some highly interesting discoveries.

Radio News, April 6, 1925.

William Stephenson and George Walton's mechanical system for transmitting still and moving images consisted of a pair of rotating discs with slots arranged around the periphery. The discs could be rotated either in the same or opposite direction, depending on the number and disposition of the slots and the relative speed of the two discs. At the transmitter (top left) a lens projected an inverted image of the subject between the overlapping discs, allowing apertures formed at the intersection of the slots to traverse the image. A second lens focused the pinhole of light created by the slots onto a light sensitive cell. (Note the similarity of the outward appearance of the cell to the BTH device mentioned earlier.) The varying current from the light cell and a disc speed control signal were then transmitted simultaneously to the receiver. A similar arrangement of rotating discs at the receiver (bottom left) was illuminated by an powerful arc lamp. The intensity signal was fed to a light control shutter while the speed control signal maintained synchronism between the two sets of rotating discs at the transmitter and receiver. The resulting image was then projected by means of another lens onto a white diffusing screen. Their synchronizing patent, GB213654, described in detail how synchronism could be maintained for both AC and DC drive motors in the receiver.

Stephenson and Walton also described an arrangement for the transmission and reception of natural colour images. At the transmitter there were three light sensitive cells each responding to one primary colour, whist at the receiver there were three corresponding light-controlled shutters each activated by currents from one of the light cells. There is no record, however, of whether such a system was ever actually built.

Their system is comprehensively described in an article based on an interview with Walton and published in the April 6, 1925 issue of the American journal Radio *News*. A full transcript of this article can be found in Appendix IV.

Improved Light Cell

The standard photo-sensitive device in use in the early 1920s with apparatus for the electrical transmission of images was the selenium cell. Whilst this produced a usefully high output proportional to the level of the incident light, it suffered from a significant lag in its response time when tracking rapid changes in intensity, particularly rapid transitions from light to dark. This severely limited the maximum speed at which images could be scanned and hence transmitted.

William Stephenson was widely reported in the popular press as having developed a faster alternative to the selenium cell. His improved system received widespread acclaim, but, surprisingly, no patent for any form of light cell under either Stephenson's or General Radio Company's name seems to exist.

At the time Stephenson was developing his improved system, the British Thomson-Houston Company, a subsidiary of the American General Electric Company had recently patented a vacuum tube based light cell. The device was described in British patent GB190218, issued on December 12, 1922.

The BTH light sensitive cell was based on a design first developed by the American General Electric Company. Through a rather convoluted, but not inconceivable connection, Stephenson may well have been aware of the British Thomson-Houston cell. The Cox-Cavendish Electrical Company, by way of their X-ray medical equipment business, had substantial experience in the manufacture of comparable vacuum devices. Cox-Cavendish was a contract manufacturer for British Thomson-Houston wireless receivers in 1922 and it is quite possible that Cox-Cavendish could have produced at least prototypes of the new light cell. Certainly, support for this can be seen in the drawing of the transmitting apparatus reproduced in the 1925 *Radio News* article[14] by Stephenson's co-worker, William Walton. The light cell appears outwardly to be very similar to the BTH device.

The General Electric cell was described by T. Thorne Baker in his seminal work *"Wireless Pictures and Television"*, published in 1926, but curiously he made no mention of either BTH or William Stephenson.

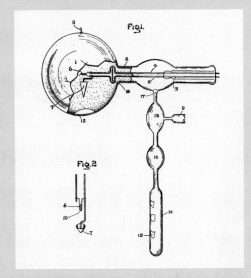

Extract from British patent GB190218 awarded to British Thomson-Houston Company.

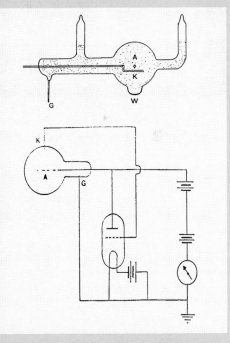

The General Electric light-cell and associated circuit: Light passing through the quartz window, W fell on the anode, A. The shaded parts were silvered onto which was deposited a layer of potassium, sodium or rubidium. The electron stream flowing from cathode, K produced a current in response to the illumination. Guard ring, G prevented leakage of the interior surface of the cell.

T. Thorne Baker: Wireless Pictures and Television, 1926.

General Radio Company
and Mechanical Television

The Radio Times, September 19, 1924.

In Canada, before moving to London, William Stephenson had reportedly been engaged in the development of mechanical scanning techniques for the electrical transmission of pictures. In 1924 he was granted, jointly with the engineer George William Walton, two patents related to mechanical scanning and synchronization of rotating bodies for the wireless transmission of still and moving images. Over the next few years, several other patents were issued jointly to General Radio Company and Walton, but these all concerned radio, not television, technology.

General Radio Company apparently exhibited television apparatus at their premises in Regent Street in September 1924. Eclipsed by John Logie Baird's mechanical television systems, however, little is recorded on the extent of General Radio Company's progress towards a working apparatus.

The "Live" Connection

The Wireless Trader, March 1924.

Product Design and Marketing

The earliest receivers manufactured by General Radio Company in 1922 and 1923 exhibit a strong North American design influence. The vertical control panels and the internally mounted valves, accessible by a hinged cabinet lid, were typically American in style. There can be little doubt that Stephenson relied on his knowledge of receiver design from his native Winnipeg, which would have been heavily influenced by American products. A seemingly small detail, but the inclusion of a headphone jack socket on the panel of General Radio Company's valve receivers and amplifiers was not standard British practice at that time. Separate terminals for connecting headphones or the loudspeaker were the norm. The headphone jack was a much more common feature on equipment produced across the Atlantic.

These early products carried a large, oval, blue and gold transfer confirming that General Radio Company was affiliated with Stephenson's other engineering interest, the Cox-Cavendish Electrical Company. Advertisements for 1922 indicate that the Company was operating from the Cox-Cavendish business address in Great Portland Street, London. By early 1923, General Radio had apparently moved to larger manufacturing premises in Harlesden (also operated by Cox-Cavendish) and by 1924 General Radio Company had opened retail premises in Regent Street, London. The association between General Radio and Cox-Cavendish ended when the latter went into liquidation in May 1924 although Cox-Cavendish was not formally wound up until December 1926.

In the Company's first years, a well-staffed marketing department expended considerable effort in creating an imaginative and constantly changing array of advertising material. This is evident from the fact that virtually every technical journal and wireless magazine featured advertisements for General Radio Company products throughout 1923 and 1924. Furthermore, the content of these advertisements was continually refreshed with meticulous attention to detail and graphic design. This emphasis on publicity at General Radio was clearly ahead of its time, at least as far as the embryonic wireless industry was concerned.

The product range at this time extended from simple, inexpensive crystal sets to luxury multi-valve cabinet receivers priced at well over one hundred pounds. Portable valve receivers, a novel idea for the period, were also featured. Headphones and loudspeakers figured prominently in the Company's literature, along with an extensive array of wireless components for the home constructor.

From the outset, Stephenson recognised the benefits of nurturing long-term relationships with dealers and distributors. The Company's *General Radio Dealer Policy* provided retailers with a written guarantee of support with merchandising and advertising of products in return for 'pushing' General Radio sets. In retrospect, it is ironic that Stephenson encouraged dealers in 1924 to look forward five and ten years when selecting a line of wireless apparatus, warning that traders who handled *"passing makes"* would suffer an *"unprofitable experience"*. In the event, General Radio Company was to be liquidated just four years later!

The pace of change in the industry meant that General Radio Company's receivers of 1922/1923, like those of other manufacturers, became obsolete very quickly. What is puzzling is that there seems to have been a period of inactivity after these first sets came to market. In an interview for the March 1925 issue of *The Wireless Trader*, Stephenson claimed that sales records continued to exceed his *"most sanguine expectations"*, asserting that he firmly believed that the next winter's sales would *"eclipse all records in the (wireless) industry"*. However, for much of that and the following year, the only products to be found in the Company advertisements were its headphones, loudspeakers and miscellaneous, small components.

In 1925, the company occupied premises at Radio Works, 22/23 Allsop Street, London, N.W.1. The introduction of a line of so-called '*unit*' receivers in that year appears to have been largely unsuccessful. Outwardly, these models retained many of the features of the earlier sets and must have begun to look old-fashioned, even by the standards of the day. By 1926, the range of products was considerably simplified and consisted primarily of just two-valve and three-valve receivers. Whilst this simplified approach to the product line remained the Company's policy until it went out of business in 1928, the last generation of receivers did see the introduction of several innovative features. Updated designs for 1927 saw the introduction of an internal loudspeaker – one of the industry's first sets to be self-contained. At the same time they offered a revolutionary (and risky) new battery technology to replace the conventional accumulators commonly used for heating the valve filaments.

ALL-BRITISH WIRELESS EXHIBITION
September 30-October 7, 1922

General Radio Company. (Stand No. 26).

The apparatus exhibited on this stand included short wave receiving sets and amplifiers specially arranged for easy manipulation. The finish of these instruments was very attractive, particularly the condenser and variometer scales, which were of nickelled metal and slightly raised. An efficient type of variometer of low self-capacity was to be seen, and was much appreciated by experimenters. It was built on a wooden frame, and had a maximum coupling between its two windings, thus providing a tuning adjustment over a wide range.

A special feature was a very beautiful multivalve cabinet receiving set. The pressing of a button provided on the front of the panel put the set into operation. To the wireless enthusiasts it was as beautiful inside as it was out.

A number of components, in particular high frequency and low frequency inter-valve transformers, were shown, of unique design.

General Radio Company *Aristocrat* six-valve receiver.

Report of *The All-British Wireless Exhibition*, Horticultural Hall, Westminster, September 30 – October 7, 1922.

The Wireless World and Radio Review, October 14, 1922.

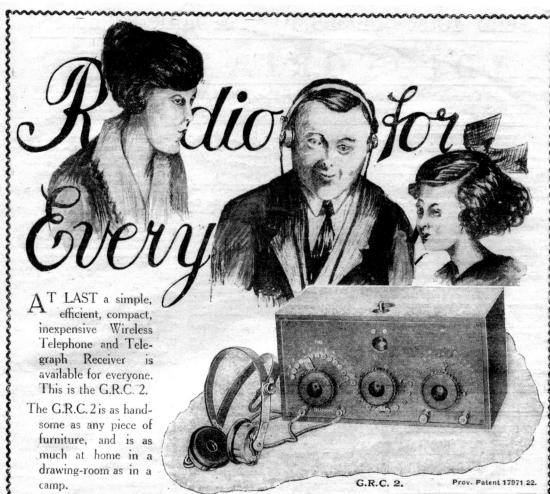

Radio for Every

AT LAST a simple, efficient, compact, inexpensive Wireless Telephone and Telegraph Receiver is available for everyone. This is the G.R.C. 2.

The G.R.C. 2 is as handsome as any piece of furniture, and is as much at home in a drawing-room as in a camp.

Tuning is so simple that any member of the family can learn to use it in a few minutes. Complete instructions are included. No batteries are required.

The apparatus comprises a highly sensitive Detector, entirely enclosed, Tuning Inductance, Variable Condenser, Fixed Condenser, and G.R.C. 24 Unitone 4,000-ohm Radiophones complete. Also G.R.C. 102 Complete Aerial Equipment. In fact, everything necessary to "listen to the world."

G.R.C. 2.   Prov. Patent 17971 22.

PRICE ONLY
£6 - 6 - 0

At your nearest Radio Shop.

Dealers and Distributors :— Know from whom you are buying. Exclusive Agencies now being allotted. Write or wire for territory.

MANUFACTURED BY

GENERAL RADIO COMPANY

Affiliated with

The Cox-Cavendish Electrical Company, Limited,

Scottish Branch : **EDINBURGH.**   105, Great Portland Street, LONDON, W.I.   *Northern Branch :* **BRADFORD.**

One of the earliest advertisements by General Radio Company for the *G.R.C.2.* crystal receiver. The monocled general had not yet made an appearance.

Popular Wireless Weekly, July 22, 1922.

ROADCASTING has gone through its trial stages and survived. The Radiophone has become institutional, won for itself a definite place in the home, and risen from the stature of a scientific toy to the proportions of a great force for good in both the fields of recreation and education. Amazing technical progress has linked arms with the genius that has guided the steady improvement in scope and quality of the programmes of the air.

A decade of progress has been crowded into a year.

HOME RECEIVING SET.

CRYSTAL RADIO RECEIVER.

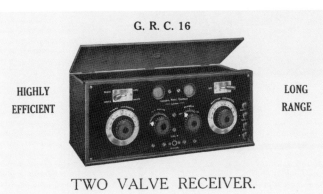

TWO VALVE RECEIVER.

TWO VALVE AUDIO AMPLIFIER

Four of the receivers and amplifiers shown in this 1923 catalogue. *"Broadcasting from America has been received on the G.R.C.16."*

"The Royalty of Radio"

General Radio described their luxurious cabinet receivers as the "*Royalty of Radio*". The Pleasure Time, The Country Home and The Aristocrat. An incongruous combination of 1920s technology and classic furniture design?

Home Installation
and Free Service Calls

In 1926 and 1927, General Radio advertised that the Company would install its two-valve receiver anywhere in the UK for just twelve pounds or a payment of one pound down and one pound per month for twelve months. The price included all accessories – "...*our engineers will fix the set just as you want it and leave it playing perfectly for you*." As an added incentive, the fee entitled the purchaser to two free service calls after installation. The same offer also applied to the three-valve receiver for a payment of four pounds down and monthly payments of one pound for a year.

In order to fulfil their obligation to install receivers anywhere in the country, General Radio assembled a team of qualified engineers on a contract basis. Advertisements for suitable engineers (young men who were homeowners or at least lived with their parents – tenants apparently could not be trusted to perform the task satisfactorily) appeared in technical journals

towards the end of 1925. The advertisements implied that the Company's part-time representatives could draw weekly cheques of from five to twelve pounds per week for the work – a very attractive prospect for young, aspiring engineers and technicians. Company literature referred to their 'corps' of several thousand trained representatives covering every city and town in the country down to the smallest hamlet. Ironically, when General Radio went into liquidation, it seems that a great many of these representatives must have been left unpaid for services rendered[15].

It was certainly an aggressive marketing approach and one not offered by other firms at the time. However, it must have been a difficult scheme to administer, especially in the more remote locations. For a company seeking a competitive advantage wherever it could find one, was it perhaps a sign that General Radio was already running into financial difficulties?

Free Installation and Service Calls

In 1926, for 20/- down and 20/- per month for a year, a prospective listener could have a General Radio two-valve receiver installed in their home. The set-up included the receiver, valves, loudspeaker, headphones and batteries. The price even included two free service calls. A similar offer was available for the Company's three-valve model at four pounds down and twelve further payments of one pound.

The installations were largely carried out by independent contractors engaged by General Radio Company specifically for the purpose.

Opposite: *Popular Wireless*, November 27, 1926.

Below: *Wireless Constructor*, December 1926.

The G.R.C. Corps of Representatives

General Radio Company advertised widely for engineers, either full-time or part-time, to install and service their receivers – the so-called *Corps of Representatives*. The ambitious concept was to cover every city, town and village throughout the entire country. Whilst it seems likely that many young men did indeed sign up for the programme, it is doubtful whether the more remote regions could have been covered adequately.

General Radio

The Standard of Excellence

Make a Profit
from your Hobby

Why not make a profit from your hobby by joining our Corps of highly successful Representatives

IN YOUR SPARE TIME.—You can secure a sound and profitable position which offers a permanent occupation in your own district with ever-increasing returns; and can be handled either in your spare time or as a whole time job. The network of our Corps of Representatives will soon cover nearly every town and village in the country.

RELIABLE MEN WANTED.—At present we require reliable men in certain districts where we are not fully represented. Applicants must be able to furnish good references and have the necessary experience to demonstrate and instal sets.

Write to our Agency Department for fuller particulars.

For years the Trade Mark, "General Radio," on a wireless installation or component has been accepted as a guarantee of quality, efficiency, and advanced design. The new catalogue of complete sets, components, loud speakers, headphones, and transformers, etc., is now ready and may be obtained free on request.

General Radio

GENERAL RADIO Co. Ltd., Radio House, 235 Regent St., LONDON, W.1

4

Chronicle Wireless Guide, Fourth Edition. Allied Newspapers Ltd., Manchester.

YOU CAN EARN MORE MONEY NOW!
Competent men wanted Spare-time or Full-time work.

A few vacancies still exist for competent men to represent us in certain districts where we are not at present fully represented.

Applicants must be capable of making a first-class job of installing wireless sets; have selling ability and initiative; be able to provide satisfactory references.

This is a splendid opportunity for the right men to make a large income or substantially supplement their present one. Full or spare-time work will be accepted. Many of our Representatives draw weekly cheques of from £5 to £12 a week for part-time work.

The unprecedented demand for the popular and efficient General Radio sets has necessitated our increasing the staff and doubling production *several times over* in the last few months, and a great number of our Representatives in all parts of the country have doubled and trebled their incomes at the same time. Further great developments in the Company are taking place every week and present unique opportunities for highly remunerative work for able and enthusiastic men.

All applications will be regarded in confidence.

Apply to our Service Department.
GENERAL RADIO COMPANY LTD., Radio House, 235, Regent Street, W.1.

Wireless World and Radio Review, March 16, 1927

Wireless for the Blind

In 1926, General Radio offered owners of crystal sets a trade-in allowance of one pound towards the purchase of one of the Company's new valve receivers. Initially the offer was restricted to "*certain types of set*" – which probably meant General Radio's own receivers – but by early 1927 the offer was opened up to any crystal set. Since headphones had to be exchanged along with the crystal set, the offer was not quite as good as it sounded at first, but then again a brand new set of headphones was included (along with a loudspeaker) with the new valve receiver.

At some point, it was decided that the crystal sets taken in exchange for valve receivers should be donated to blind listeners. The returned crystal sets were overhauled by General Radio engineers and any necessary repairs made. Installation in the home of the blind recipient, including the erection of a suitable aerial was carried out at no cost. People exchanging their old crystal set could nominate the future recipient or leave the decision to General Radio. It was a wonderful public relations exercise for General Radio and, like their free valve set installation service, was a task that no other manufacturer ever undertook, relying on the Company's contract workforce of installers around the country who apparently volunteered their time for the cause. It is only speculation, but one wonders if the General Radio management gave any incentives to its representatives to encourage them to volunteer for this unpaid work.

The General Radio plan ended in May 1927. It predated Winston Churchill's well publicised 'British Wireless for the Blind Fund' begun at Christmas 1929 which provided blind persons with a wireless receiver free of charge. In addition to monetary donations to the fund, many manufacturers donated sets to the appeal, but by this time General Radio was no longer in existence. The idea behind the fund is generally said to have occurred in 1928 to a Captain Sir Beachcroft Towse, a Boer War hero who had lost his sight at the Battle of Magersfontein. It is not inconceivable however, that given Stephenson's many interactions with Churchill during the mid-1920s in the former's developing Intelligence role[1], the earlier General Radio scheme might well have had an influence on the launch of Churchill's fund a few years later.

The Radio Times was produced in Braille for the benefit of blind listeners. The first issue was published on, May 6, 1927.

RADIO NOTES AND NEWS

Free Wireless for the Blind

THE House of Commons was dramatically stirred by the first reading of the Bill to provide free wireless licences for the blind. Captain Ian Fraser, the sightless M.P., walked up the floor of the House handed in the Bill, and in a brief speech he asked for the support of all parties, in the hope that the Bill would become law by Christmas. By tense silence during the ceremonial, and by warm cheers at the end, the House marked its approval of the measure – and the man.

Popular Wireless, November 27, 1926.

Trade In Your Old Crystal Set

Wireless, June 12, 1926.

In the summer of 1926, General Radio Company introduced a generous offer published in *Wireless* magazine. The company proposed to accept any crystal set (plus headphones) in exchange for a one pound credit towards the purchase of a valve receiver. There was, however, a limitation on the offer in the fine print – to take advantage of the promotion, only *a certain number of sets* would be accepted. Exactly which sets were eligible and whether they had to be General Radio's own crystal receivers was not clear.

In a later repeat of the same offer published in *The Radio Times* in the Spring of 1927, it was disclosed that the exchanged crystal sets were to be donated free of charge by General Radio to blind listeners and installed in their homes, also free of charge. At this later date *any* crystal set was eligible for the promotion.

HAVE YOU A CRYSTAL SET?

WE ALLOW YOU £1 *for it*

". . . . Wireless is the only type of entertainment the blind can enjoy on equal terms with you . . ."

YOUR CRYSTAL SET GIVEN TO THE BLIND

That is what happens to your set. When we receive it, we put it in sound working order and include a complete new Aerial equipment. Then our Engineers will install the set in the home of a blind person who is unable to afford the joys of Wireless.

All the sets will be given *free* and the installation carried out *without any charge whatsoever* to the Recipient, whether in the large city or the most remote hamlet.

With your co-operation, we hope to install sets in many thousands of homes of the blind.

General Radio Company Limited is the only Organisation that can undertake a task of this magnitude, and its great corps of Representatives who operate in all parts of the country are together with Headquarters Organisation voluntarily and gladly undertaking the free supply and installation of sets for the Blind.

NOTE—*You may nominate to whom you would like your set given or you may leave it to us to install it in a home selected by ourselves or recommended by one of the Blind Associations.*

WHY not exchange your crystal set for a Loud Speaker valve set ? We need not emphasize the advantages—you know them !

For three weeks only we will accept in part exchange any type of crystal set with 'phones and allow you £1 off the price of a General Radio Loud Speaker Set. [Note. A new pair of 'phones is supplied with the General Radio set as well as a Loud Speaker.]

Wonderful value. The powerful General Radio two valve Loud Speaker set in its handsome polished Walnut case is easily the best radio value obtainable. The simplicity of operation enables everyone to obtain *full, pure Loud Speaker volume* in any location.

Nothing to pay for 4 weeks ! When purchasing the set on our instalment plan your crystal set takes the place of the initial £1. So you have *free enjoyment of the set for 4 weeks.*

Normal Price	Part Exchange Price
£12 Cash or £1 down and 20/- a month for twelve months.	£11 Cash, or 20/- a month for twelve months only.

Nothing else to Buy. All General Radio sets are sold complete. *Everything* is included—full-size Loud Speaker ("Hearthside" model), a pair of Headphones, two special type Dull Emitter Valves, Accumulator, 100-volt Battery, complete Aerial equipment, all Cords and Plugs—and the royalty is paid. Every set and every part is backed by the full guarantee of General Radio Company Ltd., the pioneer radio manufacturers in Great Britain.

Free Installation. Every General Radio set is installed *free of charge* in the home of the purchaser *anywhere* in England, Scotland, Wales and Northern Ireland. One of our own Engineers will fit it up just as you want it—demonstrate it—and leave it playing *perfectly* for you.

Coupons are given with each set, entitling you to free service *after* purchase. No other organisation gives this service. It is unique and ensures that *you cannot buy a General Radio set that does not give you perfect satisfaction.*

ONLY TWO MORE WEEKS!

Send the COUPON NOW

"Provides ample volume of reception in any location."
Wireless Times, Sept. 1926.

"Winning golden opinions for the quality of its reception and simplicity."
Morning Post, 11-9-26.

This COUPON *is worth* £1 TO YOU

To GENERAL RADIO CO. LTD.,
Radio House,
235 Regent Street, W.1.

Please post me catalogue of General Radio Loud Speaker sets and details of how I may receive an allowance of £1 for my old crystal set by allowing it to be given and installed entirely free of charge in the home of a blind person.

NAME ....
ADDRESS ....
TOWN ....
COUNTY ....

(Block letters please)

R.T. 22/4/27.

General Radio

GENERAL RADIO COMPANY LTD., RADIO HOUSE, 235 REGENT STREET, LONDON, W.1.

The General Strike

The general strike of May 1926 marked a milestone in the development of the British Broadcasting Company. By maintaining a degree of independence from the Government, its credibility as an autonomous organisation strengthened its standing as a national institution. In the absence of newspapers, the BBC – with five regularly scheduled news bulletins each day – became the key instrument to disseminate information to the population at large. The signal strength of the local BBC stations was actually increased during the strike to ensure that as many listeners as possible, particularly those in known marginal reception areas, could receive the news bulletins. The incoming news material to the BBC was broadcast daily as a lead article[5], having been first edited by William Stephenson's old friend Gladstone Murray, who provided his own appreciation of the situation.

Encouraging widespread circulation of the content of the wireless bulletins, the BBC allowed many of the bulletins to be posted in public places. Handwritten copies were often to be found at the local high street wireless retailer. Never one to miss out on an unexpected business opportunity, a situation such as this played to Stephenson's intuitive strength in public relations. General Radio Company circulated some 80,000 printed newssheets from their Regent Street premises summarizing the latest BBC bulletins. Remarkably, these were distributed on the streets within just half-an-hour of the actual broadcast[4].

One can be sure that General Radio's timely sharing of the latest news was intended not only to serve the public interest, but also to generate increased interest in the Company's products. General Radio, like many other manufacturers of wireless sets, would undoubtedly have experienced a marked upturn in sales during the strike.

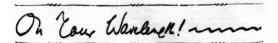

THOSE who, a few weeks ago, were ready to argue that interest in wireless matters had already reached saturation point, and were inclined to take a gloomy view of the future of the industry, must now hold a very different opinion. It is difficult to estimate the number of new wireless sets that were installed during the general strike.

It is equally difficult to estimate the true value of the part played by the B.B.C. during those days of crisis. By disseminating official news at frequent intervals each day, the B.B.C. kept the general public in constant touch with the progress of events, and so reassured the nervous element against undue pessimism.

In short, the broadcast service was for the time being invested with new and grave national responsibilities. The manner in which these were carried out has enhanced the already high reputation of those in charge, who deserve the grateful thanks not only of the wireless public, but of the community at large.

Amateur Wireless and Electrics, May 22, 1926.

Cartoon by David Low, *London Star*, May 1926.

Armoured cars protecting a food convoy on its way to London's Hyde Park.

The Illustrated London News, May 15, 1926.

RADIOLYMPIA
September 24th – October 1st 1927.

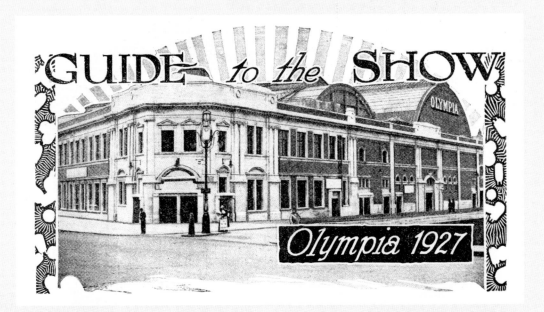

GENERAL RADIO COMPANY, Stands 45-48.

The standard two-valve receiver has been completely redesigned, and includes several interesting features. The circuit arrangement comprises a regenerative detector followed by a transformer-coupled L.F. amplifier; reaction is controlled by two moving coils operated through a regenerative gear. Waveband change is by means of a switch which eliminates a part of the aerial coil for short-wave reception.

The valves are of a new type, having double "V" filaments with an external connection. When one filament is broken, or when its emission fails, the other may be put into circuit. The consumption is slightly over 0.1 amp at about 1.4 volt. The holders are of interesting design, with spring contacts to the pins and a single-turn helical phosphor-bronze spring as a shock–absorber. There is no solid dielectric between the pins.

The loudspeaker, with a 4-inch metal cone, is included in the cabinet, on the front panel of which are mounted two edgewise dials (for tuning and reaction), an "on-off" switch, and a wave-change switch.

The Wireless World and Radio Review, September 28, 1927.

The Sensation of the

The greatest

THE FILONATOR

is supplied with every General Radio Receiving Set. The Filonator can be *recharged instantly in your own home* simply by inserting refill tablets supplied. More economical, efficient, permanent and reliable than any accumulator. None of the usual inconveniences of accumulators—*No acids*, No fumes, simple and safe.

THE NEW VALVES

Standard equipment with the new General Radio Receiver. Operates at full efficiency on *only* 1.4 *volts*, with " power valve " results, and has a *double filament* designed to the specification of General Radio Research Engineers, by the famous Valve Manufacturers, Messrs. Mullard Radio Valve Company Limited. The Valve Holders are a patented Anti-vibration type and have the *lowest interelectrode capacity* of any valve holder on the market.

THE TUNING UNIT

The Tuning Unit in the new General Radio Receiver is quite unique. The " Astatic Vario-Coupler " is tuned by a Die-cast S.L.F. Variable Condenser with constant vernier control. This is *the most sensitive and selective* Tuning Instrument in any Receiver.

The LOUD SPEAKER

The new patented " Magnetic-Cone " Loud Speaker is a revelation in perfect reproduction. Embodying entirely new fea-

tures, it is *only six inches* in diameter and produces volume and tone superior to the large unsightly horn speakers. It is fixed inside the Cabinet.

THE AMPLIFIER

The Amplifier in the General Radio Receiver is an improvement of the well-known and widely-used General Radio Transformer-Coupled Audio Amplifier, and is responsible to a large extent for the amazing purity and volume of reproduction.

**STANDS
45, 46
47 & 48**

1928 MODEL GENERAL RADIO CABINET RECEIVERS are ENTIRELY SELF-CONTAINED and are transportable.

The Cabinet is made of first quality genuine hand-polished English Walnut.

NO INCREASE IN PRICES

2-Valve Set, absolutely complete and installed free. Cash price, £12.

Deferred payment terms of 20/- down and 12 monthly instalments of 20/- are still available.

One of the very last advertisements – characteristically bullish to the end.
Popular Wireless, October 1, 1927.

Radio Exhibition!
advance since September 1923

GENERAL RADIO ✶ PRESENTS

A NEW RANGE OF
GENERAL RADIO RECEIVING SETS
incorporating the following exclusive patented features

NO ACCUMULATOR!

NEW DOUBLE-POWER DOUBLE-LIFE VALVES

THE PATENTED "ASTATIC VARIO-COUPLER"
which provides perfect selective tuning with ONE control

"MAGNETIC-CONE" LOUD SPEAKER BUILT INTO SET

MANY OTHER EXCLUSIVE FEATURES

FREE INSTALLATION
FREE SERVICE

This Coupon (or a post card will do)
will bring you full particulars
without obligation—
Send it now.

To
General Radio
Company Limited,
Radio House,
235 Regent St., London, W.1

Please send me full particulars without
obligation.

Name

Address

Town

County

E30.

The Company Liquidates

The end of 1924 marked the passing of protectionism for the British radio industry. From January 1, 1925 dealers were at liberty to sell foreign radios. Increased competition forced British manufacturers to lower their prices even though they were still burdened with a Marconi royalty of 12/6 per valve holder. This royalty was to remain in place until 1929 and must have had a significant impact on the profitability of companies like General Radio.

By 1927, General Radio Company appears to have run into serious financial difficulties. Reduced profits from a limited product line were no doubt aggravated by the ambitious infrastructure put in place by Stephenson in anticipation of a world-wide business. The Company's publicity department alone must have been a huge drain on resources.

The Company had borrowed, by way of debentures, a total of £27,500 between October 1923 and June 1927. Of this amount, only £7,500 was ever settled – £1,500 in November 1926 and a further £6,000 in June 1927. The business being generated by General Radio Company during 1927 must have been insufficient to service the outstanding £20,000 debt (somewhere around £800,000 to £1,000,000 in 2010 terms) plus any interest that was accruing on the loan. On February 16, 1928 the debenture holders, Redeemable Securities Trust Limited – later 1st Co-operative Investment Trust Limited – obtained a court order to have a liquidator appointed to wind up the Company's affairs.

A resolution to cease operations was entered on March 30, 1928 – "the Company, by reason of its liabilities, cannot continue its business, and that it is advisable to wind up the same". The liquidator was duly appointed by the court and a final, winding up meeting of the Company was held on October 11, 1928.

As a side note to the story of the liquidation of General Radio Company, the process had the distinction of establishing legal precedent in regard to the entitlement of contractors to receive financial compensation – in this case the corps of individuals engaged by General Radio to install and service receivers in the home[20]. In the case of "General Radio Company Limited and First Co-Operative Investment Trust Limited versus The Company", two of these service engineers by the names of Lewis and Bailey claimed that they were due a payment, but the courts seem to have taken the position that these contractors served the Company's customers, not the Company itself and consequently were not entitled to any payout from the monies remaining at the time of the Company's liquidation. Further, they were not covered by the 'Workmen's Compensation Act' since neither Lewis nor Bailey could be classified as labourers. This was, in the opinion of the court, "an inapt description of a person who procured purchases and completed them by installation". Just how many contractors had been lured by the tempting opportunity presented to them in 1925 and 1926 can only be a matter of speculation, but it seems there was a risk of enough disgruntled ex-installers and service engineers making trouble to warrant a court action.

And so the Company, formed just five years earlier under the leadership of William Stephenson with the ambition to dominate wireless receiver development in Great Britain, ceased to exist. A common enough story in the fledgling wireless industry of the time and one that would be less noteworthy were it not for the celebrated directors who had been involved in the formation of General Radio Company:

Sir William Samuel Stephenson who was the inspiration for James Bond, arguably the world's best-known and best loved spy character.

Frederick Wissler, creator – for better or worse, depending on your taste – of the savoury spread, Marmite and succeeded at General Radio and as Managing Director of Marmite by his son William.

Donal Morphy, founder of the legendary home appliance company, Morphy-Richards, a household name at home and abroad.

In retrospect, General Radio was a relatively large and seemingly well organised company that should have succeeded. One can only speculate why an illustrious team like this could have allowed such a failure to occur, apparently so easily. Between them, they surely could have raised additional capital to keep the enterprise going had they believed it was capable of becoming a profitable concern. Perhaps the founders simply felt that there were better opportunities to follow?

Little was ever put into print afterwards detailing the circumstances that had led to the demise of General Radio Company. Undoubtedly the directors preferred to look to the future and to overlook past mistakes. In the case of William Stephenson and Donal Morphy, of course, the future was to ultimately prove very successful by any measure. General Radio Company would be relegated to the sidelines of their respective stories.

Epilogue

Following the demise of General Radio, William Stephenson did have one last flirtation with the radio industry. In October 1928 he joined the board of the newly formed Symphony Gramophone and Radio Company. It was, however, destined to be a brief affair. The enterprise, which arose out of the ashes of the famous company of A.J. Stevens of Wolverhampton, was in operation for just 18 months before being wound up.

Stephenson assumed the position of Managing Director under the influential chairmanship of Colonel Sir Arthur Holbrook, the Member of Parliament for Basingstoke from 1920 to 1929. Stephenson's hand in the Company is evident from the confident advertising in such prestigious journals such as *Punch* and *The Illustrated London News*. Several of Symphony's products were targeted at the very high-end of the market that was just developing for the newly fashionable radiogram. The '*All-Electric Symphony Radio-Gramophone*', for example, retailed at £115 to £125, reminiscent of Stephenson's bid to produce expensive Cabinet Receivers during his early years at General Radio. Plagued by manufacturing problems and a limited market for such exclusive products, the Company was wound up in 1930.

If six years of running General Radio had left Stephenson in any doubt about the rigours of the domestic wireless business, his subsequent experience with Symphony must have clarified matters for him. He never again returned to the wireless industry.

Symphony stock certificate dated December 20, 1928 showing Sir Arthur Holbrook and William Stephenson as Directors of the recently formed Company. Symphony was to be Stephenson's last foray into the field of domestic radio.

Punch, November 6, 1929.

A Radiophone in Every Home.

SHEET MUSIC AND RADIO

RADIO SHOW

**Third Annual Exhibition of Receiving Sets,
Broadcasting Apparatus and Radio Appurtenances
Generally Opened This Week
in the Coliseum, Chicago.**

Big Foreign Exhibit.

In the foreign section are displays by the principal
radio concerns of England, France, Germany, Italy,
and Japan. Among the noted foreign companies
represented are the Acme Production Company of
Birmingham, England; the Institute of Radio
Research, Tokyo, Japan; The Ando Kaku Radio
Company, Yokohama, Japan; Burndept, Ltd., of
London; the Deutsche Telephonwerke &
Kabelindustrie of Berlin; **the General Radio
Company, Ltd., of London**; the M-L Magneto
Syndicate Coventry, England; the Societa Generate
Radio de Bologna, Italy; Pathe Freres, and G.
Pericaud, of Paris.

Presto - The American Music Trade Weekly, November 22, 1924.

General Radio Company Receivers, 1922-1928

Crystal Sets

The Company's first crystal receiver is thought to have been a small pre-broadcast sloping panel model. The set, marked simply *GRC*, featured an internal loading coil for long-wave reception, this being brought into circuit by a front panel switch. Before broadcasting formally began in Britain, in November 1922, there was little for the public to listen to. This set, however, would have enabled them to tune in to the continental, long wave stations. The Paris time signals transmitted from the Eiffel Tower on 2,600 metres, or the Sunday afternoon concerts from The Hague on 1,085 metres, were popular alternatives. Relatively crude by comparison with the Company's later sets, its construction typified the almost 'amateur' appearance characteristic of smaller firms in these early days. This first crystal set was probably introduced just prior to the time Stephenson first assumed an interest in the company.

The earliest product known to have been advertised by General Radio Company was the *G.R.C.2* – a pre-broadcast crystal receiver introduced in mid-1922. The *G.R.C.2* was a much more robust crystal set of distinctive appearance. Unusually, the cat's-whisker detector contact was located inside the cabinet and could be viewed through two small circular windows, one in the front panel and the other on top of the cabinet. Tuning was by coarse and fine tapped inductance in conjunction with a variable condenser. The overall design of the receiver, which could be operated in either an upright or a horizontal position, exhibited strong North American influence mentioned previously. Described by the manufacturer as *"handsome as any piece of furniture, and as much at home in a drawing-room as in a camp"*, the set was something of a break from conventional British crystal set designs of the day. The receiver carried the company's characteristic blue oval transfer showing collaboration with the Cox-Cavendish Electrical Company of Great Portland Street, London. At the time of its introduction the *G.R.C.2*, complete with headphones and accessories, was priced at six guineas. putting it in the upper echelons of the crystal sets of the day. By November 1922, the price had been reduced to five guineas.

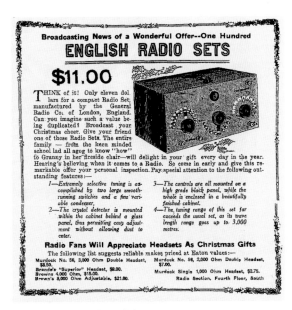

Advertisement by T. Eaton & Company,
Winnipeg Free Press, December 8, 1922.

In December 1922 this set was being advertised in Canada by Eaton's Department Store in the Winnipeg Free Press. One hundred receivers were offered at the 'bargain' price of just eleven dollars, in time for the upcoming Christmas shopping season. The exchange rate in 1922 of approximately five Canadian dollars to the pound supports the claim that it was indeed a bargain price. Certainly, General Radio would have been concentrating on the development of new models for the domestic market at around this time, and so it is probable that these 'bargain' sets were actually old stock that was being offloaded overseas. At the same time, this would have had the additional benefit of getting the Company's name known in Stephenson's native Canada.

It may also be that the company did not wish to submit the *G.R.C.2* for approval under the newly introduced British Post Office regulations for broadcast receivers, fearing, perhaps, that the receiver would not have met the requirements. At the time, the only requirement for crystal sets was that they should have sufficient tuning range with both a 30 ft. and a 100 ft. aerial attached.

In the early 1920s, Eaton's Winnipeg store on Portage Avenue dominated the local retail market with over 8,000 employees. The population of Winnipeg reportedly spent half of their shopping dollars at Eaton's and, on a good day, ten percent of them might visit the store! Occupying some twenty-one acres, Winnipeg was also the centre of the retailer's mail order business.

William Stephenson's choice of Eaton's to sell off his excess receivers in 1922 was clearly a strategic business decision. As a Winnipegger, he must have been well aware of the potential of the operation.

Interestingly, the only example of the *G.R.C.2* known to the authors was found in a Winnipeg antique shop in around 1990. This example is therefore likely to be one of those one hundred bargain sets sold by Eaton's Department Store around Christmas 1922.

A *G.R.C.4* crystal set with variometer and variable condenser tuning, covering 250-650 metres, was introduced in late 1922 or early 1923, priced at a more affordable £3 15s. 6d. (No reference to a model *G.R.C.3.* has been discovered, nor are any extant examples known). The *G.R.C.4* receiver employed the same cabinet and a similar, internally-mounted detector arrangement to that used in the *G.R.C.2.* The terminals were insulated with ebonite and now included an extra pair for connection to an external note magnifier for loudspeaker operation. The use of the same cabinet as the *G.R.C.2* may well indicate that left-over stock was being utilized. The *G.R.C.4* was the first General Radio product to carry the BBC/Post Office approval mark and was given the relatively early registration number, 132. This would suggest that approval had been obtained in late 1922

or at the beginning of 1923. The approval number was stamped onto a metal plate fixed to the cabinet.

The *G.R.C.5* receiver, a smaller, variometer-tuned crystal set of 1923, has survived in the greatest numbers of any of the General Radio products. At £2 5s. 6d., the *G.R.C.5* was the least expensive of the company's receivers and was competitively priced with other manufacturers' instruments of similar quality. According to the Company's literature, the set was particularly popular with Boy Scout Troops *"on the move"* where it was used for *"reception of instructions from Headquarters."* It was produced in two similar designs, an early version housed in a cabinet with a brass key-lock in the lid and a later model with a traditional latch. (The purpose of the lock is open to speculation – possibly to prevent servants or children of the house from interfering with the cat's-whisker or the dial setting.) The two versions can also be distinguished by the engraved BBC approval mark on the panel of the earlier set, while the later one has a stamped brass plate on the lid. The two variants are otherwise mechanically identical, but the later one includes a condenser wired across the headphone terminals. They do, however, carry two different Post Office registration numbers of 140 and 142, respectively. It would appear that the inclusion of the condenser was enough to warrant re-registration with the authorities and the issuing of a new number. Such a small modification was not likely to have ever been discovered, but illustrates the ethical practices in place at General Radio Company at the time. It is highly doubtful that many of their competitors would have been so diligent in complying with the cumbersome government regulations. Apart from a non-standard cat's-whisker/galena crystal assembly (presumably of the company's own design) the overall design of the set is otherwise unremarkable.

Another crystal set called The "Rex" employed the same circuit as the later G.R.C.5 but was constructed in a slightly larger, open mahogany cabinet. This model also carried the registration number, 142 and was likely introduced in late 1923 or early 1924.

In common with the first valve receivers and amplifiers, the early crystal sets featured the unique, fluted 'Anticap' tuning dials engraved with the Company's initials. These nickel-plated brass dials could be earthed to reduce hand-capacity effects and so improve stability when tuning the set. Like most of General Radio's innovative components the dial was available individually, for use by amateur constructors. Unfortunately, the 'G.R.C.' engraved on the dial is sometimes responsible for the misidentification of amateur-built receivers of the period being attributed to General Radio Company.

The last of the General Radio Company's crystal sets was the G.R.C.6, produced during 1924. The enclosed and miniaturised 'cartridge' detector is not found in any of the company's previous products. Controls on either end of the cartridge assembly allowed the crystal and the cat's-whisker to be rotated independently – the latter being mounted eccentrically, so that as much of the surface of the crystal as possible could be covered. The detector was almost certainly of the company's own design, but for some reason it does not appear to have been offered as a stand-alone component. Tuning was by a variable condenser also of the company's proprietary design. An internal socket for a standard plug-in type coil, accessible by means of a hinged lid on the top of the cabinet, allowed a wide range of wavelengths to be received by substitution of different coils. Extraordinarily slim, the tuning condenser was about the same thickness and diameter as a standard tuning dial and, being surface mounted, it took up no room behind the panel. Whilst providing a wide range of tuning capacitance (0.00001 to 0.001 microfarads), it had the disadvantage of requiring two complete revolutions of the dial to cover the full range. This meant that any position of the dial actually corresponded to two different wavelengths. In 1925, the variable condenser was offered as an individual component (G.R.C.63), priced at 10/. Surprisingly, although carrying a provisional patent application number, no issued patent for the condenser has been found.

This crystal set is thought to be a very early General Radio Company receiver, likely produced in 1922. It bears the initials GRC engraved on the front panel and the variometer and tuning dial are of the Company's own design. (The permanent detector shown is a contemporary replacement. It is of a type commonly retrofitted to crystal receivers in the mid-1920s as an improvement over the original, temperamental cat's-whisker detector.)

This, the only known example of *G.R.C.2*, was found in an antique shop in Winnipeg, Canada. The set was likely bought new from T. Eaton & Co. Ltd. of Winnipeg around Christmas 1922.

G.R.C.2 crystal receiver.

G.R.C.4 crystal receiver.

"An excellent crystal set which can be used in either upright of flat position. The detector is entirely enclosed. Very highly finished in polished mahogany."

Wireless Apparatus and Accessories, A.J. Dew & Company, 1923.

"The G.R.C.5 is an ideal receiver for general purpose. Boy Scout Troops use it extensively while on the march for reception of instructions from Headquarters."

General Radio Company catalogue, 1923.

G.R.C.5 crystal receivers. Left: GPO No.140. Right: GPO No. 142.

The Rex was an open cabinet version of the *G.R.C.5* carrying the GPO registration number 142.

The *G.R.C.6* was the last of the General Radio Company's crystal receivers.

Early 'Unit-System'

Among the first products to be offered by General Radio were the *G.R.C.11* long-range tuner and *G.R.C.12* detector-capacity unit. When combined with the company's matching *G.R.C.13* low-frequency and *G.R.C.14* high-frequency amplifiers these components formed a complete wireless receiver. Such 'unit-systems' were quite typical during the first years of broadcasting and were offered by several of the major manufacturers. Favoured by the technically minded for their flexibility (much as component hi-fi systems were to be half a century later), they must have seemed unnecessarily complex to the average listener.

Early Valve Receivers and Amplifiers

The company introduced one- and two-valve receivers in late 1922 or early 1923. The single valve set, the *G.R.C.18*, priced at £6 6s. 0d. was advertised only briefly in February 1923. The model does not appear to have been produced in any significant volume.

By far the most widely advertised set of the period was the two-valve *G.R.C.16* receiver, carrying the Post Office registration number, 2030. Claimed as being capable of receiving American broadcasting, the receiver employed a single stage radio-frequency amplifier plus a detector and covered wavelengths up to 600 metres. It appears that the set was never adapted for long-wave reception although, confusingly, a panel switch marked *'LONG WAVES'* and *'SHORT WAVES'* was provided, but this was to accommodate different length aerials, not to change wavelengths. The headphone connection by means of a jack-plug reflected General Radio's 'trademark' American influence.

Priced at £14 5s. 0d. at the time of its introduction, the *G.R.C.16* receiver underwent continuous retail price reductions throughout 1923 – an indication of the severe competition in the market. By December of that year the set was being offered at £10 15s. 0d. Advertisements at the time featured *The General* complaining of the sale of *large quantities of foreign made radio instruments injuring the prestige of British Wireless*. The stark and rather 'scientific' appearance of the sets probably added to their competitive woes.

Although the receivers were self-contained, matching two- and three-valve audio amplifiers continued to be offered – the *G.R.C.13* and *G.R.C.14*. (The latter model number had previously been used on the Unit-System high-frequency amplifier which appears to have been discontinued.) The amplifiers were of similar dimensions to the *G.R.C.16* receiver and the terminals were located to align with those of the receiver when they were mounted side by side. The two units could be neatly joined by short interconnecting strips.

A three-position panel switch on the *G.R.C.13* allowed either valve to be used separately or in tandem – a handy feature if, or more likely when, one of the valves failed. The company's signature headphone jack socket on the panel automatically disabled the loudspeaker terminals when the phones jack was inserted. For increased volume in a large room or hall, the three-valve *G.R.C.14* could be used as a 'power amplifier' by fitting high-output valves designed to operate at *"300 volts or more"*.

If it's a G.R.C.
it's a better set!

G.R.C.
RECEIVING EQUIPMENT

is so far in advance that it is recognised to-day as the standard by which all Radio Receiving Equipment is judged.

Look for the makers' name-plate when you purchase radio apparatus. If it bears the name "GENERAL RADIO COMPANY" you are assured that the instrument represents the highest efficiency combined with the most advanced design——at a price that is always reasonable.

Any G.R.C. Dealer will be pleased to demonstrate so that you can judge for yourself the superiority of G.R.C. APPARATUS.

There is a G.R.C. Radiophone for every purse and purpose.
Our CATALOGUE will interest you—Write for it—it's FREE.

GENERAL RADIO COMPANY

TWYFORD ABBEY WORKS, ACTON LANE, HARLESDEN, N.W.10
Telephone : Willesden 3055 (3 lines).   *Telegrams :* " Milliamp, Phone, London."

Showrooms :
105, GREAT PORTLAND ST., W.1.

Branches :
EDINBURGH and BRADFORD.

G.R.C. apparatus will be shown by Messrs. Mottershead & Co., at the Manchester All-British Wireless Exhibition, 17th-24th March. We are also exhibiting at the Ideal Home Exhibition, Olympia, 1st-24th March.

Modern Wireless, March 1923.

G.R.C.
EFFICIENCY

G.R.C. 13
2-Valve Amplifier.

G.B.C. 27
LOUD
SPEAKER

G.R.C. Amplifying and Loud Speaker Equipment will convert any receiving set into an efficient Loud Speaking Receiver, and at a reasonable cost. No additional batteries or accumulators are required and no alterations to the receiver are necessary.

Any owner of a G.R.C. Set can prove to you that G.R.C. Equipment is the "Royalty of Radio." Our free book " A Radiophone in Every Home " tells why. Write for it—NOW.

**We manufacture
a complete range
of parts, too.**

GENERAL RADIO COMPANY

TWYFORD ABBEY WORKS, ACTON LANE, HARLESDEN, N.W.10

Telephone : *Willesden* 3055 (3 *lines*).
SHOWROOMS : 105, *Great Portland Street, W.1.*

Telegrams : " *Milliamp*, 'Phone, London,"
BRANCHES in all cities.

The Wireless World and Radio Review, May 26, 1923.

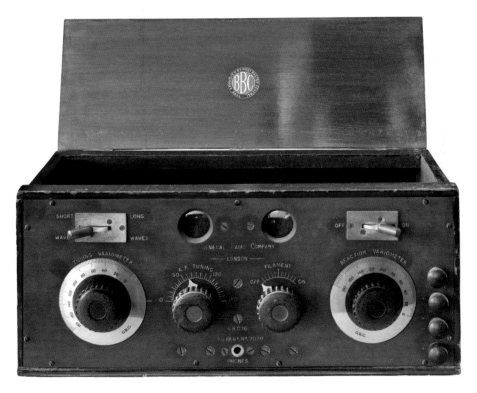

The *G.R.C.16* two-valve receiver carrying the GPO registration number 2030.
G.R.C.16 kindly loaned by the Mike Kemp.

The *G.R.C.13* two-valve amplifier carrying the GPO registration number 3012.
G.R.C.13 kindly loaned by the Amberley Museum and Heritage Centre.

Cabinet Receivers

Three high-end receivers, described by the company as the *Royalty of Radio* were offered in late 1922 – *The Pleasure Time, The Country Home* and *The Aristocrat*. These elegant 'drawing-room' receivers certainly carried retail prices more suited to royalty than the pocket of the average person, ranging from around £70 to £169*. Featuring inlaid, cross-grained, French-polished cabinetry and silk loudspeaker cloth these elaborate sets were exceptionally stylish pieces of furniture in their own right. *The Aristocrat* was displayed at the 1922 *All-British Wireless Exhibition* held at the Horticultural Hall, Westminster, London. Extolling the set's sophistication, a review of the exhibit in *The Wireless World and Radio Review* also made a point of the fact that the receiver could be brought into operation by "the touch of a button" on the front panel. Along the same lines, a report of the March 1923 *Daily Mail Ideal Home Exhibition* at London's Olympia published in *The Wireless Trader* noted the receiver's *'almost automatic control'*.

The Pleasure Time was offered in a stylish 'Sheraton-style' cabinet with loudspeaker above the panel and a double-door cabinet beneath. General Radio literature touted this model as especially attractive to flat-dwellers who desired an attractive piece of furniture in place of a more traditional wireless set. The Company's frame aerial was fitted inside the cabinet. As its name implied, *The Country Home* was designed for the country house, club or hotel with its appropriately styled Jacobean cabinet and barley-twist legs.

Whilst they incorporated an enclosed horn loudspeaker, the five- and six-valve receivers, sporting seven or eight dials, must have been tricky to adjust, and their performance was probably matched by less expensive models available from competitors. It is hard to imagine that many of these sets ever left the factory – perhaps the words of Churchill some twenty years later can be adapted here – *"Never before was so much paid for so many (valves) by so few"*!

A four-valve model housed in an inlaid mahogany 'smoker's-cabinet' was also advertised in 1923. *The Hearthside*, was simply the *G.R.C.16* receiver and *G.R.C.13* amplifier mounted in a single cabinet along with a built-in loudspeaker. The 47 guinea price tag represented a considerable mark-up over the original separate units.

It is not clear how long these sets were on the market. A guide to the September 1926 *National Radio Exhibition* at Olympia does list *'various cabinet receivers'* on display at the General Radio Company stand . It is doubtful whether these were updated designs and would quite probably have been an attempt to sell off the original models. It is equally doubtful whether any of these sets have survived.

Such models would have been obsolete within a matter of a few years and in all likelihood these magnificent receivers would have been dismantled for parts or worse consigned to the family bonfire.

* By way of comparison, in 1922, a top-of-the-line Austin 7 family car would have been priced at around £152 – less than General Radio Company's Aristocrat receiver.

General Radio's *Aristocrat* cabinet set was featured in Harmsworth's *Wireless Encyclopedia* of 1923 as a fine example of a receiver which could be considered a 'musical instrument'. The interior view shows the six-valves and other components mounted on a swinging front panel allowing ready access for servicing.

Harmsworth's Wireless Encyclopedia, 1923.

A Radiophone in Every Home

G.R.C. 58. "ARISTOCRAT"

The "ARISTOCRAT" is the finest Receiving Instrument made. Constructed of inlaid cross-grained mahogany, the "Aristocrat" Cabinet is a wonderful example of the Cabinet-makers' art. The panelling, fretcut, and inlay all combine to picture radiation.

This Radiophone is the leader of a complete line of wireless apparatus which is constructed throughout in our Factory.

It is a six-valve receiver with Loud Speaker contained inside the Cabinet. Ballast tubes automatically control the filaments.

Tuning is accomplished by the rotation of a single dial, and it is merely necessary to press a small silver button on the panel to put the receiver into operation.

G.R.C. 56. "PLEASURE TIME"

The "PLEASURE TIME" model is worthy of its name and will give many happy hours to its fortunate owner. The upright Sheraton Cabinet is of distinctive design and must not be confused with Receiving Sets which are made to fit cheap gramophone cabinets.

This model should particularly appeal to flat dwellers who wish to have an attractive piece of furniture when buying a Receiving Set.

An outdoor aerial is unnecessary, and the Loud Speaker is an integral part of the instrument.

G.R.C. 57. "COUNTRY HOME"

The "COUNTRY HOME" model is a five-valve self-contained Radiophone complete with Loud Speaker, mounted in a Jacobean Cabinet of pleasing design.

This is an ideal Receiver for the Country Home, Club, or Hotel. Simple to operate and highly efficient, the reception of voice and music is exceptionally good and the volume may be regulated from a whisper to a greater volume than that ordinarily obtained from a gramophone.

These are just a few examples representative of the G.R.C. line.
Our free book "A Radiophone in Every Home" tells the whole story. Write for it.

The "*Aristocrat*," "*Pleasure Time*" and "*Country Home*" were amongst the most expensive wireless receivers on the market with retail price tags between seventy and one hundred and sixty nine pounds. Such outlays were several years' pay for an average working person and completely unreachable for all but the wealthiest.

Modern Wireless, May 1923.

AN EXAMPLE OF

G.R.C.

SUPERIORITY

Price Complete ready to operate:

47 Guineas.

Includes self-contained Loud Speaker, Headphones, Accumulator, Batteries, Valves and complete aerial equipment.

A postcard brings our free book—
"A Radiophone in every Home."
Write for it
NOW

The model illustrated is the **G.R.C.52** " Hearthside " 4-Valve Cabinet Receiving Set.

Completely self-contained, the " **Hearthside** " is fitted with Amplifiers and the finest Loud Speaker.

The french-polished inlaid mahogany cabinet contains compartments for the headset and batteries. Valves are enclosed and the entire operation is controlled by rotating the panel dials.

This Receiver will be found suitable for telephony up to at least 100 miles on the Loud Speaker and greater distances when using headphones.

Before buying ANY Receiving Set or Component compare it with a G.R.C. product.

There is a G.R.C. Set to suit every purse and purpose—designed by up-to-date Radio Engineers of experience—made throughout in a modern Factory—thoroughly tested before dispatch—and sold to you at reasonable price.

GENERAL RADIO COMPANY

TWYFORD ABBEY WORKS, ACTON LANE, HARLESDEN, N.W.10

Telephone: Willesden 3055 (3 lines).
SHOWROOMS : 105, *Great Portland Street,* W.1.

Telegrams]: *" Milliamp, 'Phone, London."*
BRANCHES *in all cities.*

The *"Hearthside"* was a four-valve receiver (one high-frequency amplifier, one detector, two low-frequency amplifiers).
The French polished 'smoker's-cabinet' included a built-in loudspeaker and compartments for headphones and high-tension battery.

The Wireless World and Radio Review, May 12, 1923.

Portable Receivers

Quick to recognise the need for 'wireless on the move', General Radio introduced two so-called 'portable' receivers in 1923. These were four- and five-valve sets in a bulky mahogany cabinet that resembled a small travelling chest, complete with brass lock and leather carrying handle. Of substantial construction, the open lid of the receiver could be used as a writing stand. Two innovative features for the time were an internal frame aerial wound inside the case and a 'quick-release' front panel held in place by specially designed clips, presumably to make valve replacement and other repairs more practical when out and about. There was no internal speaker – headphone jacks on the panel allowed three pairs of headphones to be connected. The price of portability, though, was high. In 1923, the smaller, four-valve model was priced at a hefty £48 15s. 0d.

'Portable' Receivers

The "Ubiquitous" Portable Receiver is particularly suitable for use in pleasure cars, on camping trips, or in fact for any purpose where it is desired to have a highly efficient receiver which is entirely self-contained and easily portable.

G. R. C. 55

PORTABLE RECEIVER.

General Radio Company was one of the first companies to offer 'portable' receivers. The term portable was, of course, in the context of the technology of the early 1920s when portability meant the inclusion of a carrying handle on what was otherwise a bulky and heavy piece of equipment. The high price meant that these receivers would have been enjoyed by only the wealthy.

Second Generation 'Unit-System' – 1925

Under the banner of *'Indoors or Outdoors, One Valve or Eight'*, General Radio introduced a new line of 'Unit-System' receivers in early 1925, with individual units designated *G.R.C.501* to *504*. These were a range of vertical cabinet, single-valve assemblies consisting of a receiver, high-frequency amplifier, low-frequency amplifier and power amplifier. The units could be assembled in a variety of combinations by means of plugs and sockets, with as many stages of high- and low-frequency amplification as desired. According to their literature, the company intended up to eight of these single valve units to be used together, although it hard to imagine that very many listeners would have wanted such a complex and expensive arrangement.

The receiver unit, *G.R.C.501*, priced at £9 0s. 0d., was a compact set, employing reaction, and could be used as a stand-alone receiver with a range of about 100 miles on headphones. If a longer range was wanted, the high-frequency amplifier, *G.R.C.502*, could be plugged into the side connectors of the receiver. A panel switch marked *'DETECTOR'* and *'AMPLIFIER'* was moved to the latter position if the high-frequency amplifier was employed. There was no need to unplug the aerial or the earth connections to the receiver.

The low-frequency amplifier, *G.R.C.502*, and power-amplifier, *G.R.C.503*, likewise were fitted with side plugs for attaching to the receiver and for multiple stages of amplification. Outwardly, the *G.R.C.502* and *G.R.C.503* were identical with exception of grid bias battery sockets on the panel of the power amplifier unit. The amplifier units were priced at £6 0s. 0d. each. In principle, the low-frequency and power amplifier units could be joined together in any combination.

The company's uncompromising publicity department asserted that with this new range of products, General Radio was *"still the standard of quality in receiving sets"*. But with their old fashioned porthole viewing windows for observing the valve filaments, the units were already somewhat dated in their design even by the standards of the day. Both the receiver and the high-frequency amplifier featured the company's proprietary slim-line condenser. This was advertised as the 'Express Condenser', but was essentially the same device as had been introduced in the *G.R.C.6* crystal set.

Given their out-dated design and considering the lack of surviving examples, it is likely that these Unit-System components were not particularly popular with the listening public.

Third Generation Receivers – 1926

Breaking with the design of the first generation of receivers and the Unit-System, two new and updated receivers were introduced in 1926 – the two- and three-valve *General Type 15* and *General Type 17*. Described in the sales literature as *"an article of furniture which will harmonise with the finest surroundings"*, the *Type 15* was a compact two-valve receiver housed in a polished walnut case with a tuning range from 250 to 2,400 metres. Otherwise similar, the *General Type 17* was a three-valve version of the same set incorporating an additional stage of audio amplification.

The tuning was by means of the Company's proprietary condenser enclosed within the dial. The extended wavelength coverage of the new sets was achieved with an internal coil tapped at three points, the wires being taken to sockets. A flexible lead with a wander plug could be inserted into the appropriate socket on the coil to allow reception of the desired waveband. The design required that the listener gain access to the inside of the set to change wavebands. It was a rather cumbersome arrangement, although the patented cabinet design[16] embodying a hinged front panel permitted relatively easy access to the internal coil. The hinged panel, sprayed black with distinctive gold highlights, did have the added advantage that access to valves and other components was relatively straightforward. Intended for reception of the local BBC station at loudspeaker strength, the front panel continued to incorporate the 'trademark' American-style jack connection for attaching the loudspeaker. The *General Type 15* and *Type 17* receivers were both supplied with the General Radio Hearthside speaker. Insertion or withdrawal of the jack plug automatically switched the batteries 'on' or 'off', allowing the user to simply *"push one plug into its socket to secure perfect loudspeaker reception."*

The *General Type 15* and *Type 17* receivers were the subject of a favourable review in the September 1926 edition of *Wireless Magazine* in the run-up to the first *National Radio Exhibition* held in the first two weeks of the month at the New Hall Gallery, Olympia. Both featured in the magazine's *Guide to the Best Valve Sets*. The three-valve model was described as a *"well-made set with performance in every way equal to its smart appearance."* The two-valve receiver was hailed as a powerful receiver for home entertainment. Excellent loudspeaker reception of the BBC's London station 2LO was reported some twenty miles from the transmitter, while the Newcastle, Birmingham and Dublin stations could be heard clearly on headphones. The same model, however, was given a rather less complimentary assessment in an extensive three-page review in the respected journal *Wireless World and Radio Review* in March 1927. The article commented on the *"metallic ring"* in the sound quality that could not be eliminated by adjustment of either the receiver or the loudspeaker. The redeeming feature, though, was the receiver's reasonable price of £12. 0s. 0d., including valves, batteries, headphones and aerial and earth equipment all packed in a special case. The three-valve *Type 17* was priced at £15. 0s. 0d.

General Radio Unit-System

In March 1925, General Radio announced a 'Unit-System' receiver. Single-valve units comprising receiver, low-frequency amplifier, high-frequency amplifier and power amplifier could be assembled to produce a variety of receiver configurations. Each unit had side connections to mate with an adjoining unit to provide a contiguous assembly. A typical, high-end system might have consisted of one or two high-frequency amplifiers, receiver, two or three low-frequency amplifiers and a power amplifier. Such complex systems were, however, rapidly becoming obsolete as wireless became an entertainment medium for the non-technical listener.

The Wireless Trader, March 4, 1925.

This version of the *Type 15* two-valve receiver of 1926 features a distinctive gold sprayed metallic front panel.

The three-valve *Type 17 was outwardly similar to the two-valve model.*

PATENT SPECIFICATION

Application Date: Jan. 20, 1926.   No. 1634/26.   **268,475**

Complete Left : Oct. 20, 1926.

Complete Accepted : April 7, 1927.

PROVISIONAL SPECIFICATION.

Improvements in the Construction of Cabinets and Framework of Wireless Receiving Sets.

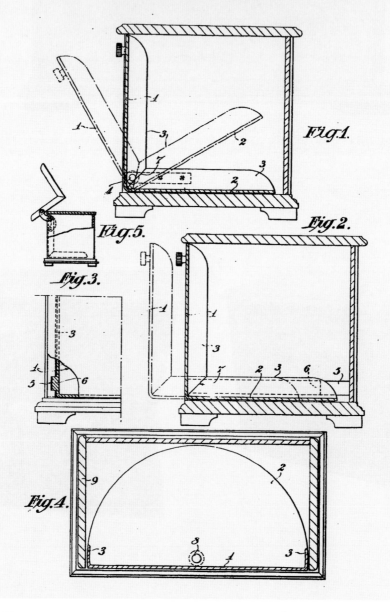

Extract from patent GB268475, showing drawings of the hinged front panel design of the General Radio Type 15 receiver.

A Complete Loud-speaker Receiving Installation for £12.

Tested at a distance of approximately four miles from 2LO and sixty five miles from Daventry, ample loudspeaker volume was obtained from both stations, and on the former station the reaction control had to be reduced to zero and the set slightly detuned to prevent overloading the last valve. Several Continental stations were also received on the 300- to 500-metre waveband, but the somewhat uneven distribution of capacity over the condenser scale increases tuning difficulties when searching for distant stations.

The loudspeaker volume is excellent for two valves, but the quality was characterised in the specimen under test by a peculiar metallic ring which could not be eliminated by any adjustment of the controls

However, it is difficult to be hypercritical in view of the extremely reasonable price of the whole outfit, and the performance of the set as a whole is sure to give satisfaction in the market for which it is intended.

"...satisfaction in the market for which it is intended." – a rather lukewarm review of the *G.R.C. Type 15* receiver.

The Wireless World and Radio Review, March 9, 1927.

The National Radio Exhibition
September 4th – 18th, 1926.

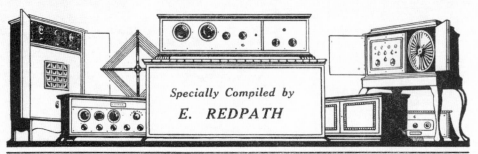

STAND 103, GENERAL RADIO COMPANY LIMITED

A distinctive and powerful two-valve set in open-fronted cabinet of polished walnut, the front panel being of metal with black crystalline finish. Essentially a home-entertainment set, extremely simple to install and to operate, it is capable of giving excellent loudspeaker results from the local broadcasting station (20-25 miles distant), and, with a little careful adjustment of the single tuning dial and the reaction or volume control, good results in telephones from stations at considerable distances. Switching on and off is done by merely inserting or withdrawing the loud-speaker plug.

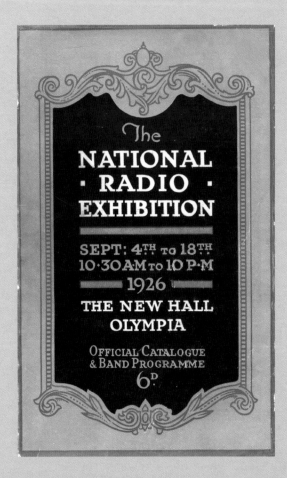

Wireless Magazine, September 1926.

General Radio Type 15 Two-valver.

General Radio
The Standard of Excellence

Famous People
who have broadcast recently

H.M. The King, H.R.H. The Prince of Wales & other members of the Royal Family. The Rt Hon Stanley Baldwin & other members of Parliament, Lord Mayor of London, Melba, Tetrazzini, Sir Harry Lauder, Straccari, Chaliapin, Albert Sammons, Paderewski, Dame Clara Butt, Kennerley, Rumford & many others.

Two-Valve Receiver
TYPE 15

SUPPLIED absolutely complete with all accessories to ensure immediate and perfect reception, including:—

Broadcast Receiver, G.R.C. 15.
Loud Speaker, "Hearthside" full size model, G.R.C. 29.
Headphones. "Lightweight" Type G.R.C. 20.
Two Special New Patent Dull Emitter Valves.
Hundred-Volt Battery (including Special Grid Bias Taps).
Two-Volt Accumulator.
All necessary Cords and Plug.
Complete Aerial Equipment.
Royalties Paid.
All carefully packed in special case.
PRICE:—
£12 0 0 complete, or
£1 0 0 cash and
12 Monthly Payments of
£1 0 0 each.

ALL ROYALTIES PAID.
ALL BRITISH MADE.
"The General Radio Company are making it easy to get Wireless in the home."
The Star, Dec. 7th, 1926.

Three - Valve Receiver
TYPE 17

THE General Radio Broadcast Receiver, Type 17, is a three-valve Receiver of the same general construction as the Type 15, but is provided with an additional amplifier stage. This assures sufficient volume in locations at long distances from Broadcasting Stations, or where considerable volume is required, and for Halls, Public Rooms, etc.
Supplied absolutely complete with all necessary accessories to ensure immediate and perfect reception, including:—

Broadcast Receiver, G.R.C. 17.
Loud Speaker, "Hearthside" full size model, G.R.C. 29.
Headphones, "Lightweight" Type, G.R.C. 20.
Three Special New Patent Dull Emitter Valves.
Hundred-Volt Battery (including Special Grid Bias Taps).
Two-Volt Accumulator.
All necessary Cords and Plug.
Complete Aerial Equipment.
Royalties Paid.
All carefully packed in special case.
PRICE:—
£15 0 0 complete, or
£4 0 0 cash and
12 Monthly Payments of
£1 0 0 each.

1926 General Radio Company advertising brochure.

The Morning Post, 11/9/26

"A wireless set free from all complications is made by General Radio. At Olympia this set is winning golden opinion for the quality of its reception and simplicity."

The Manchester Guardian, 4/9/26

"Never before have valve sets been brought so nearly within the reach of the shallow's pockets."

General Radio
THE STANDARD OF EXCELLENCE

The Sunday Express, 5/9/26

"This great wireless firm are now introducing a new method of selling wireless sets with "service." Each set is installed free in the house of the purchaser, and periodical visits are subsequently made to see that the set is working well."

Swansong – the 1928 Models

The last of General Radio Company's receivers – the *1928 Models* – were introduced in the autumn of 1927. By October of that year, the company had relocated its head office and works to 42a, Bravington Road, London, W.9. It is not known if the new models were ever produced at this location, but it appears that this was the intent.

Completely redesigned, the two- and three-valve sets were introduced to the public at the *Radiolympia* show held between September 24th and October 1st at the New Hall Gallery, Olympia, London and organised by the Radio Manufacturers' Association. Constructed in a hand-polished, solid mahogany cabinet with a copper faceplate and mesh loudspeaker grill, the outward appearance of the sets, at least, was several years ahead of the competition. Industry leading features included magnifying glass windows to improve the visibility of the edgewise dial scales and push-pull on/off and wavechange switches on the front panel. A battery compartment was incorporated beneath the steel chassis.

Perhaps the most advanced feature of the new products was the incorporation of an internal loudspeaker – the *Beco* marketed by British Electrical Sales Organisation of London. The *Beco*, introduced in 1925, was the first British moving-iron, cone loudspeaker and its use in a self-contained receiver was a sophisticated concept for the day. Although described as 'self-contained', the set did not in fact feature a built-in aerial.

Tuning was by means of dual 0-100° and 0-200° worm-drive dials coupled to the Company's proprietary 'astatic vario-coupler' and *Polar* diecast variable condenser*. A piece in the March 9, 1927 edition of *The Wireless World* notes " ... the uneven distribution of capacitance made tuning difficult sometimes."

A newly developed internal low-tension accumulator known as the *Filonator* that could be refilled in the home eliminated the need for conventional recharging. The *Filonator* itself was re-charged by making up two solutions obtained by dissolving special tablets in tap water and adding a new zinc electrode; tablets and zinc electrodes were provided with the set and additional supplies could be purchased from wireless dealers.

Promotional literature stated that the new sets were to be supplied with either the Mullard Type *P.M.0.* valve or a 'new valve' produced by the Electron Company. Although the literature was ambiguous, the implication was that these valves were designed especially for use with the *Filonator*. The specified valves incorporated double filaments designed to operate even if one of the filaments burned out. Requiring less than 1½ volts (compared to 2 volts for standard accumulator types), they seem to have been similar to dry-cell types of the period. Curiously, though, there is no evidence that Mullard ever supplied such a valve in any volume and nothing is known of the Electron Company type.

Although not directly affecting the type of valves employed, the patented General Radio anti-vibration valve holders[19] employed curved internal connecting strips that ran from a particular valve pin around to the diametrically opposite tag. As a result the grid tag was adjacent to the valve's anode pin and the anode tag was adjacent to the valve's grid pin. It was an unusual arrangement that must have caused considerable confusion when the time came time to service the receiver. A write-up in the March 9, 1927 edition of *The Wireless World* notes that the set could not be transported with the valves in-situ as the sprung valve holders tended to allow excessive lateral movement.

Coincident with the introduction of their 1928 models, the Company acquired the business of Radiobats, a wireless battery manufacturer. The purchase included the company's manufacturing equipment, patents, processes and trademarks. The Radiobats high-tension battery was to be offered as standard equipment with all General Radio receivers. Whether or not it was intended to merge the manufacturing is not known. Between 1924 and 1928 Radiobats operated from premises at 18, Snow's Fields, Bermondsey, London, S.E.1., although after the acquisition all communications with Radiobats were handled by the Head Offices of General Radio Company. Further, Radiobats finances were immediately combined with those of General Radio – presumably Stephenson regarded in-house battery production as a means to reduce costs and improve profitability. Radiobats ceased business in 1929, about a year after the winding up of General Radio Company.

Despite all of their new features, the *1928 Models* were offered at the same retail price as the earlier *Type 15 and Type 17* receivers. Unfortunately the 1928 model year was to be cut short by the company's decision to cease operations in the first months of the year. As a result, very few of the company's latest and greatest receivers could have ever made it into the homes of the listening public.

* Details of the construction of the receiver courtesy of Jonathan Hill.

The centre of attraction – new double-life valves, one control tuning, no accumulators, no price increase, installed free!

The Wireless World and Radio Review, October 12, 1927.

Three-valve receiver of 1927. This model included a self-contained moving-iron cone
loudspeaker – an unusual feature for the time when external loudspeakers were still the norm.

"The loudspeaker is especially interesting – 5 inches diameter, moving iron with an aluminium cone and rear adjustment... The rather complicated variometer drive is neatly carried out and gives symmetry to the layout."

Norman Jackson, May 1982.

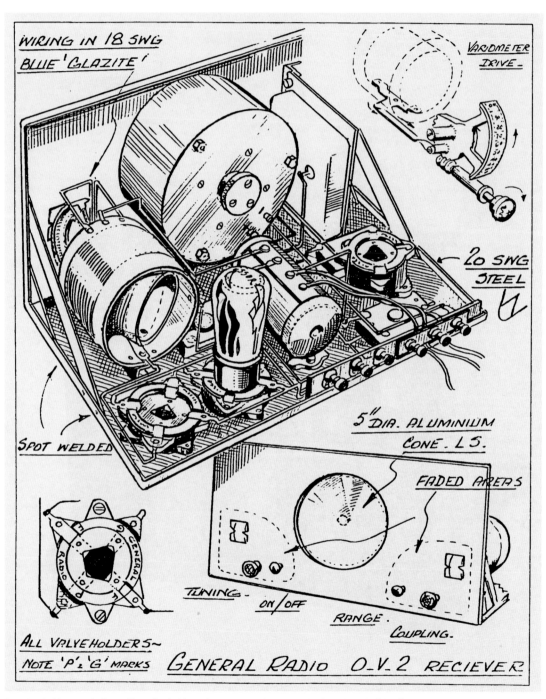

Drawing by Norman Jackson. The valve holders show apparently reversed grid and anode (plate) markings.
The markings are actually correct, as each tag in this patented anti-vibration design connects to its diametrically opposite valve pin.

Bulletin of the British Vintage Wireless Society, May 1982.

Radiobats Company Limited

Radiobats Company Limited was registered in October 1924 by Mark Samson of 73, Shoot Up Hill, London and Nathaniel Samson of Rochfield Road, Oxted, Surrey. Mark Samson, of Polish descent, was described variously in the company documents as a costumier or ladies' tailor and his business partner, Nathaniel Samson simply as agent. In March, 1925 two more directors joined the company's board - Leonard Levy, a Doctor of Science and William Stephenson, Managing Director of General Radio Company. The four directors are shown as owning one ordinary share each, while Mark Samson also was awarded 1,000 preferred shares.

Little is known about Stephenson's role in Radiobats or indeed of the operation of the company in general. Certainly, their products were not widely advertised. On November 28, 1927, Radiobats board informed the Companies Registration Office that in future they would be carrying on business under the proprietorship of General Radio Company, but retaining the name Radiobats. Following this, Stephenson communicated to the Registration Office at the end of December that Radiobats was 'the property' of General Radio Company and that Radiobats was 'merely a trade name'; all accounts were henceforth embedded in those of General Radio.

A General Radio Company press release in *The Wireless World* and *Radio Review* for September 21, 1927 announced that all products of the Radiobats Company, including the *Radiobat High Tension Battery*, would, in future, be obtainable as standard equipment with General Radio receiving sets. The same press release referred to the purchase by General Radio Company of the sole manufacturing and selling rights for a 'revolutionary' double-fluid electric cell (to be later named the *Filonator* by General Radio) previously manufactured by Darimont Electric Batteries Limited. William Stephenson appears to have been positioning General Radio Company to produce and supply its radio batteries in-house.

Radiobats was dissolved by notice in the *London Gazette* dated April 5, 1929. Interestingly this was after the winding up of the parent company, which occurred at the end of 1928.

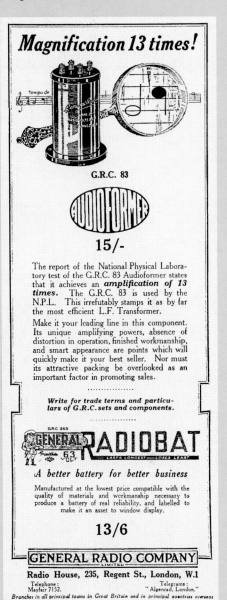

The Wireless Trader, September 1924.

Left: Entry in the list of shareholders of the British Broadcasting Company. The address for Radiobats is incorrectly shown as 18, Somerfields, Bermondsey. The actual company address was 18, Snowsfields, Bermondsey, London, S.E.1.

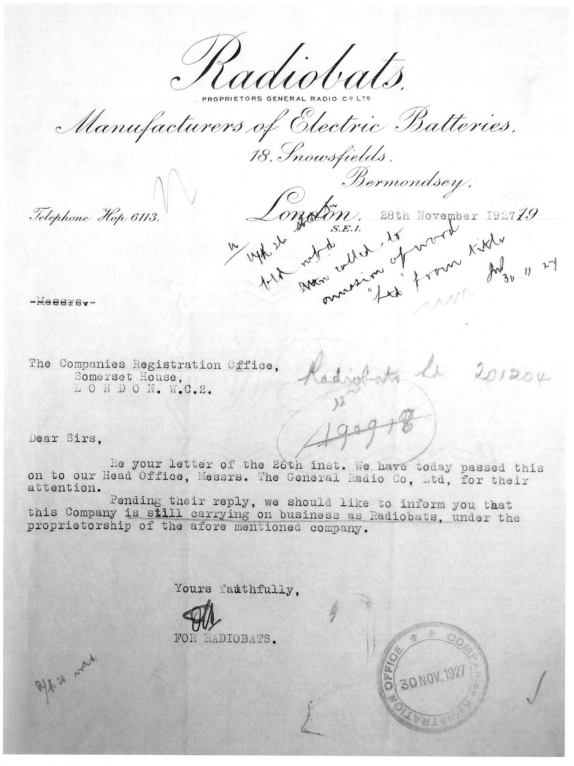

Radiobats.

PROPRIETORS GENERAL RADIO Cº LTº

Manufacturers of Electric Batteries.

18, Snowsfields,

Bermondsey,

London, S.E.1.   28th November 1927*79*

Telephone Hop 6113.

—Messrs.—

The Companies Registration Office,
    Somerset House,
    L O N D O N. W.C.2.

Dear Sirs,

        Re your letter of the 26th inst. We have today passed this
on to our Head Office, Messrs. The General Radio Co, Ltd, for their
attention.

        Pending their reply, we should like to inform you that
this Company is still carrying on business as Radiobats, under the
proprietorship of the afore mentioned company.

                Yours faithfully,

                FOR RADIOBATS.

30 NOV. 1927

Letter from Radiobats to Companies Registration Office regarding their trading status.

GENERAL RADIO COMPANY
LIMITED.
MANUFACTURERS OF WIRELESS, X RAY & ALLIED APPARATUS

Telegrams:
ALGENRAD. LONDON.
All codes used

Telephone:
WILLESDEN 3701 (PRIVATE BRANCH EXCHANGE)

Showrooms: 105, Regent St. W.1.
BRANCHES AND AGENCIES,
IN ALL PRINCIPAL COUNTRIES.

DIRECTORS:
A. MORPHY, W.E.S. WISSLER
B.H. MORPHY, D.W. MORPHY.
MANAGING DIRECTOR:
W.S. STEPHENSON.

HEAD OFFICE *and* WORKS:
1 – 42a
BRAVINGTON · ROAD
LONDON · W · 9

28th December 19 27.

C.C.Gallagher, Esq.,
Companies Registration Office,
Somerset House,
London,
W.C.2.

Dear Sir,

      In reference to your letter of the 30th
ultimo, under reference 201204, we have to advise you that
Messrs Radiobats is a property of General Radio Company
Limited and that "Radiobats" is merely a trade name.

      We would refer you to the fact that
notice of cessation was given by the old Limited Company
from whom the concern was purchased by us. You will,
therefore, appreciate that all accounts under this
heading are now embedded in those of the General
Radio Company.

      We are, dear sir,

      Yours truly,
GENERAL RADIO COMPANY LIMITED.

BY:

SECRETARY.

EB/DSA.

Letter from General Radio Company Ltd. to Companies Registration Office regarding the trading status of Radiobats.

The 'Filonator'

The *Filonator*, supplied with the last of General Radio Company's receivers, was heralded as a new generation of primary battery destined to rapidly replace the ordinary accumulator as a supply for valve filaments. Developed by the Belgian engineer, Leopold Darimont, and distributed in the United Kingdom by Darimont Electric Batteries Limited of 329, High Holborn, London, W.C.1., these unique batteries could be *"recharged instantly in the listener's home simply inserting special compressed tablets"*. In 1927 General Radio Company acquired sole manufacturing rights and christened the device the *Filonator*.

Leopold Darimont was a prolific inventor with numerous patents to his name relating to a variety of technologies, including improvements to microphones. However he seems to have been particularly devoted to advances in electric cells, with patents dating back to 1912 with research continuing throughout the 1920s. Darimont Electric Batteries Limited was registered in September 1922, with offices at 536, Salisbury House, London, E.C.2. The company's first directors included Darimont and fellow Belgian, George Hagemaus.

The company exhibited an early version of the new primary battery at the All-British Wireless Exhibition held at White City in November 1923, but there was scant reference to their products in the technical press until the acquisition by General Radio Company. During 1923 and 1924, Darimont Electric Batteries Limited was operating at 96a, Villiers Road, London, N.W.2. Telephone records show that in 1925 the company moved to Darimont Works, Abbey Road, London, N.W.10., where it was located until 1927.

According to press reports put out by General Radio Company, the batteries had been subject to stringent testing over several years before being released to the public. Those eager to dispense with their cumbersome accumulators, which required transportation to the local garage or cycle shop for recharging, had their first sight of the revolutionary new *Filonator* at the Radiolympia show in September 1927.

The chemistry associated with the Darimont's cells was complex and made use of an extraordinary array of both organic and inorganic materials – wax, powdered coke, corn starch, soap, linseed oil, chalk, kaolin, caustic soda and more. The construction was similarly intricate, requiring a number of air- and liquid-tight seals that had to remain intact throughout the life of the device. It is highly doubtful whether such a cell could ever have been made reliable enough for its intended market and no extant examples are known[*].

General Radio Company went out of business shortly after acquiring the design and manufacturing rights to the *Filonator* and it is a matter of conjecture as to what part, if any, the device played in the company's demise. Leopold Darimont, ceased to be a director of the company in 1930; Darimont Electric Batteries Limited continued in operation until a request was made to liquidate the company in April 1935.

[*] A more comprehensive description of the construction of the Filonator is given in Appendix V.

PATENT SPECIFICATION

180,120

Application Date: Mar. 16, 1921. No. 8256/21.

Complete Accepted: May 25, 1922.

COMPLETE SPECIFICATION.

Improvements in and relating to Electric Primary Cells.

I, LEOPOLD DARIMONT, of 10, rue Tete de Mouton, Anderlecht-Brussels, Belgium, a subject of the King of Belgium, do hereby declare the nature of this inven-
5 tion and in what manner the same is to be performed, to be particularly described and ascertained in and by the following statement :—

This invention relates to a two-fluid
10 primary electric battery of the kind comprising an outer receptacle containing a zinc electrode and a solution of a non-acid chloride such as sodium chloride as an exciting fluid, also an inner porous
15 vessel within which is a carbon electrode and perchloride of iron as a depolarizing fluid.

In cells of the above mentioned kind the depolarizer soon penetrates through
20 the porous vessel and covering the zinc with an insulating layer, the cell becomes useless.

It is already known in a two fluid cell for the porous cell to have its upper part
25 made perfectly impenetratable, and also for the upper part of the carbon electrode to be similarly treated. In a single fluid battery it has been proposed to add chromic acid to the exciting fluid. Further,
30 in an iron-carbon, single electrolytic battery it is known to employ perchloride of iron as a depolariser.

No claim is made to these features per se.

35 The objects of the present invention are to obviate the diffusion of the exciting and the depolarising solutions and to provide a cell which shall be hermetically closed whilst capable of being easily taken to
40 pieces if necessary and which is able to supply a current in a continuous or intermittent manner.

According to the present invention an

anti-acid material, such as powdered chalk is added to the exciting solution. 45 As the perchloride of iron penetrates through the wall of the porous vessel a chemical combination takes place between the perchloride and the chalk, forming an insoluble material which becomes 50 incrusted in the wall of the said vessel so that this latter soon acts as a porous vessel with a semi-pervious membrane. Diffusion of the two liquids is thus avoided and the zinc is protected. 55

To prevent the powder sinking to the bottom, an addition of an agglutinant is made to keep it in suspension in the exciting solution. To allow of the practical use of this exciting paste, other 60 materials are added for the reasons hereinafter set forth.

In order to prevent the semi-pervious layer being formed too deeply in the wall of the porous vessel, there is added to the 65 depolarizing solution a material that is capable of dissolving the excess deposit of ferrous material.

Moreover, to prevent the oxides and hydrates contained in the commercial 70 perchloride of iron producing insulating deposits on t
alkaline chlo
precipitating
other purpose
Further, t
oxide or hyd
occur in con
air upon t
chemical dec
ing solution,
cally closed.
To preven
of the perch
the porous
above the p

[Price 1s.]

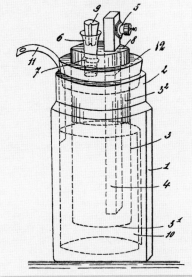

Leopold Darimont applied for a patent describing an improved primary cell as early as March 1921. Darimont's cell formed the basis of the General Radio Company's *Filonator* touted to replace the commonly used accumulator. Shown here are extracts from patent GB180120.

In September 1927, under the banner of *"Announcements of great importance to those interested in wireless"*, General Radio introduced the Filonator battery and the new valves designed for use with it. As already pointed out, the enigmatic valves do not seem to have been commonly available.

The Mullard *P.M.0* valve

The Mullard *P.M.0* never went into general production and no detailed performance data was ever published. Outwardly it resembled a typical Mullard triode of the period with a paper label around the base. Designed for use with the Filonator, it was a general purpose triode with a filament rating of 1.4 Volts at 0.14 Amps[20].

FILONATOR

DARIMONT ELECTRIC BATTERIES LIMITED beg to announce the introduction of a new type of Primary Battery which will rapidly replace the ordinary Accumulator.

These unique batteries can be recharged instantly at home simply by inserting special compressed tablets. Nothing else is necessary ! These batteries have passed stringent tests over a period of years and will now be available to the public.

The foremost Radio Manufacturers—Messrs. General Radio Company, Ltd., of Radio House, Regent Street, London, have acquired the sole manufacturing and selling rights of this revolutionary invention (which is fully patented),and after exhaustive tests in their modern Laboratories they have decided to supply this Unit as standard equipment instead of Accumulators with every General Radio Receiving Set. The name of this type of electric supply Unit is the General Radio Filonator (Patented throughout the World).

The Filonator will be on display for the first time at General Radio Company's Stands Nos. 45, 46, 47, 48, at the National Radio Exhibition.

DARIMONT ELECTRIC BATTERIES, LIMITED,

329, HIGH HOLBORN, LONDON, W.C.I.

NEW VALVE

THE MULLARD P.M.O. VALVE is so designed as to operate with the new General Radio Filonator, which supersedes the Accumulator and is rechargeable instantly in your own home, simply by inserting special compressed tablets.

These Valves require less than $1\frac{1}{2}$ volts to operate at full efficiency and are equipped with the Mullard P.M. filament.

They will be supplied with General Radio Receiving Sets.

🔊 🔊 🔊

THE ELECTRON COMPANY, LIMITED, take pleasure in announcing that they have designed and produced a new type of valve, in accordance with the specifications of the Engineers of General Radio Company, Ltd., Radio House, Regent Street. This valve is designed to operate with the new General Radio Filonator (which supersedes the ordinary Accumulator) and is rechargeable instantly at home.

The new valve requires less than $1\frac{1}{2}$ volts to operate at full efficiency and is equipped with a *double filament*. Its characteristics are practically those of a power valve. These valves will be supplied with General Radio Receiving Sets.

THE ELECTRON Co., LTD., 122/4, CHARING CROSS ROAD, LONDON, W.C.2.

The Wireless World and Radio Review, September 21, 1927.

General Radiophones

General Radiophones constitute such a remarkable stride forward in Radio Science that they are destined to revolutionize wireless phone manufacture. They are the ultimate achievement of prolonged laboratory research coupled with many years of practical experience in manufacturing.

The Wireless Trader, April 1924.

From its earliest days, General Radio was a reputable manufacturer of high-quality headphones, marketed under the *Radiophone* trade name. In 1922, before the Company was formally registered, the entrepreneurial William Stephenson forged a business relationship with Brandes of Toronto. Canadian Brandes Limited, operating out of the Great Portland Street address that General Radio was then sharing with Cox-Cavendish, seems to have been set up for the purpose of getting a foothold in the burgeoning headphone business. Canadian Brandes marketed headphones in Britain under their own *'Matched Tone'* trademark, but these were, in reality, manufactured by General Radio Company and were essentially the same product that General Radio sold as their *G.R.C.2 Radiophones.*

It is interesting to note that in June 1923, Canadian Brandes Limited, now located at 294-300 Regent Street, London, were advertising that their products bore the BBC approval stamp. There is no record, however, of Canadian Brandes ever having been a shareholder member of the British Broadcasting Company[17]. Most likely Stephenson facilitated the 'sharing' of General Radio's approval by Canadian Brandes for the headphones bearing their name. The exact nature of the relationship between General Radio and Canadian Brandes is not known, but it was undoubtedly close. Indeed, a 1923 General Radio catalogue for their full product range shows only Brandes headphones. The two companies may also have shared marketing resources. The attractive young lady featured in the Brandes advertisements, although she has not been formally identified, bears a striking resemblance to the model appearing in the General Radio Company headphone advertisements – even down to her hair-style!

In 1924 a new company was established – Brandes Limited (the 'Canadian' was dropped from the name.) A purpose-built plant known as the *Brandes Works* was opened in Slough specifically to manufacture headphones. Brandes became a bona fide BBC member in 1924 and the relationship with Stephenson and General Radio seems to have ended.

General Radio Radiophones were a mainstay of the Company's business throughout 1924 and 1925. Stephenson's patented method of adjusting the assembly during production simplified headphone manufacture and ensured that the earpieces were well balanced electrically. Promoted as *"seven ounces of sensitivity"*, the units were lightweight and as comfortable for the wearer as any on the market and, retailing at one pound per pair, they were also competitively priced. Custom ear-pads could be purchased for 1/- per pair to provide additional comfort. By March 1925, over half a million sets of headphones had reportedly been produced. All in all, they were perhaps the most successful of all General Radio's products.

7 ounces: 1 pound

- General Radiophones weigh seven ounces.

- Their price is one pound.

- If you are buying weight they are the most expensive 'phones made.

- If you are buying results they're far and away the cheapest.

GENERAL RADIOPHONES

Modern Wireless, February 1925.

Brandes Limited

Brandes, a Canadian Company founded in Toronto in 1908, became part of the American International Telephone & Telegraph Company (ITT) in 1922. For a short time, prior to the establishment in 1924 of a British headphone manufacturing subsidiary in Slough, the Canadian Brandes Company shared facilities with General Radio.

Brandes quickly expanded into the production of economically priced loudspeakers and, after the parent US company merged with the Kolster Radio Corporation of America, was renamed Kolster-Brandes. Kolster-Brandes moved into the production of complete receivers during the late 1920s. The Company enjoyed notable success in 1930 by securing a contract to produce forty thousand small bakelite receivers that were given away by the Godfrey Phillips tobacco company in exchange for cigarette coupons. There is no record of any involvement by William Stephenson in Kolster-Brandes.

Wireless World and Radio Review, February 23, 1923.

General Radiophones

General Radiophones fit any head without the adjustment of screws or nuts of any description.

GUARANTEE

These telephones have been very carefully tested before leaving our factory, and are guaranteed perfect. They will be replaced free of charge if returned to us for any fault within ten days of purchase.

GENERAL RADIO COMPANY
LIMITED
RADIO HOUSE
Regent St. LONDON.W.

General Radio Company Catalogue, 1926.

GENERAL RADIOPHONES

General Radiophones

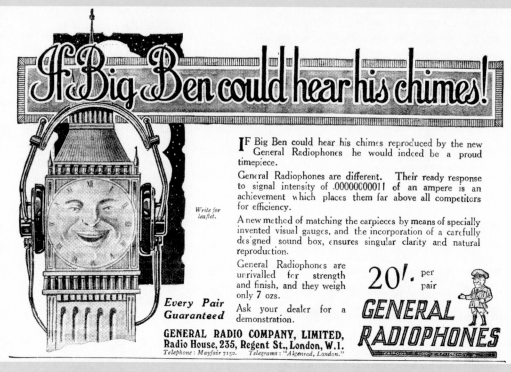

Modern Wireless, October, 1924.

General Radiophones – Seven Ounces of Sensitivity.

Brandes
The name to know in Radio

Brandes Matched Tone Radio Headphones
20/-
RETAIL

Brandes Table-Talker
42/-
RETAIL

Write for copies of this showcard.

Brandes Limited
206, Regent Street, London, W.1.
Works - SLOUGH, BUCKS.

The young lady in this Brandes advertisement bears a striking resemblance to the model appearing in General Radio Company literature for the company's Radiophones – see page 39.

Wireless Trader, April 22, 1925.

King's College
Strand, London, W.C.2.

General Radio Company Limited   January, 1925
Radio House,
235, Regent St.,
London, W.1.

Dear Sirs,

Kindly allow me to express my appreciation of your achievement in your "General Radiophones." I have frequently applied them in many exacting scientific experiments in the place of delicate galvanometers and find them an entire success.

Their extreme sensitivity, their lightness and durability combined with extreme beauty of external appearance make them an exceptionally good investment especially in view of their moderate price.

Personally, I prefer them to many makes of 'phones nearly double the price and recommend them unreservedly.

         I am, Sirs,
            Yours sincerely,

                W.L.S.   B.Sc. (1st, Hons.)

This glowing tribute from an unknown member of the staff of King's College, London was often quoted in the company literature. Solicited or not, it was impressive nonetheless.

Loudspeakers

General Radio Company produced at least five models of horn loudspeaker between 1922 and 1926. Based on the lack of surviving examples compared to those of other companies, none appear to have been particularly popular with listeners.

The earliest design, the *G.R.C.25*, known as the *Ampliphone*, was simply an aluminium horn assembly to which a pair of headphones could be attached at the base. Advertised in September 1922, the Company claimed that the arrangement provided twice the usual volume, since two earpieces were employed, not just the single driver of a traditional loudspeaker. The *Ampliphone* retailed for two guineas without headphones, which had to be purchased separately. Rather misleadingly, General Radio literature asserted that, by doubling the volume, the listener was saving half of the usual cost! The product was actually identical to a version known as the *Am-Pli-Tone*, manufactured in early 1922 in the United States and distributed by the King Corporation of New York. The relationship between the two companies is not known, but it appears that the General Radio *Ampliphone* was probably no more than a rebadged *Am-Pli-Tone*. It is quite possible that William Stephenson became aware of the King Corporation and its products in the early 1920s while he was still in Winnipeg. Certainly the business dealings of the short-lived, Stephenson-Russell Company brought him into contact with pioneering radio companies operating in the New York area at this time [3].

The *G.R.C.27* loudspeaker introduced in 1923 was an unusual arrangement in which the horn was mounted on a mahogany cabinet containing the driver assembly. A typical horn loudspeaker speaker of the day was generally supported on a small, circular metal or wooden base or stand. The General Radio unit was more sophisticated and styled to complement the Company's *G.R.C.16* receiver and *G.R.C.13, G.R.C.14* amplifiers. A single control on the front panel permitted mechanical adjustment of the driver assembly. Priced at a hefty £7 10s. 0d., it was another example of General Radio aiming its sights on the high-end of the market. It is unlikely that there was much demand for such an expensive unit. At the time, a high-quality horn speaker could be purchased for five or six pounds, whilst an average model might be about three pounds.

Two later conventional horn speakers were, rather confusingly, given the same names as the company's expensive 'cabinet' wireless receivers – the *Hearthside* and the *Pleasure Time*. Unlike the earlier *G.R.C.27* they were priced in line with equivalent models from other manufacturers, at £1 15s. 0d. and £3 10s. 0d., respectively in 1925. These straight-necked, American-style horns were reportedly fabricated from a *trade secret, composite material* claimed to eliminate any trace of *'tinny rattle'* from the reproduced sound. In general though, the style and black crystalline finish of the General Radio horns were quite similar to those manufactured and distributed by the Brandes Company whose horns were formed from compressed wood-pulp. Most likely, the General Radio horns were made of similar materials.

An enclosed speaker housed in a finely polished dark walnut cabinet, the *Aristocrat*, was offered in late 1925/early 1926, retailing at five guineas. The cabinet, measuring 15 x 9 x 9 inches, was remarkably compact considering that it contained the speaker's drive unit and an extended "folded" horn some thirty-six inches in length. The *Aristocrat* speaker was priced at five guineas.

The last of the General Radio horn speaker models was a conventional 'swan-neck' type that was supplied with the updated 1926 two- and three-valve receivers. Although the Company's literature claimed that the instrument featured a newly patented die-cast diaphragm providing *'full crystal clear volume'*, the driver unit outwardly appears to be the same as that used in the earlier, straight-necked *Hearthside* model. Otherwise, not much is known regarding the mechanical construction of this loudspeaker. Like all of the General Radio Company loudspeakers, given that so few seem to have survived suggests it could only have been produced in relatively small numbers, despite the fact that the Company supplied it as a standard unit with the 1926 receivers.

Further development of horn speakers ended with the introduction of the Company's 1927 receivers which incorporated an internal moving-iron loudspeaker. In this regard, General Radio was an industry leader, albeit for a short time until the company was dissolved in early 1928.

The General Radio Company Ampliphone was the UK version of the American Am-Pli-Tone horn loudspeaker. Headphones were clamped to the rubber pads at the base.

Twice the Volume – Ampliphones and Am-Pli-Tones

The General Radio Company's Ampliphone (G.R.C.25) loudspeaker was identical to the Am-Pli-Tone model produced in early 1922 by the King Corporation of New York. King seems to have been a trade distributor, rather than a retailer, so it is probable that General Radio purchased and remarketed the product under their own name. It is doubtful that General Radio was the manufacturer as claimed in advertisements for the product.

Designed to accept a pair of headphones clamped to rubber pads at the base of the unit, it was finished in polished aluminium with a polished nickel base and horn bell. Whether the speaker actually produced twice the volume of a conventional horn as advertised is doubtful, but it would have made a novel and compelling marketing feature of the kind that General Radio embraced.

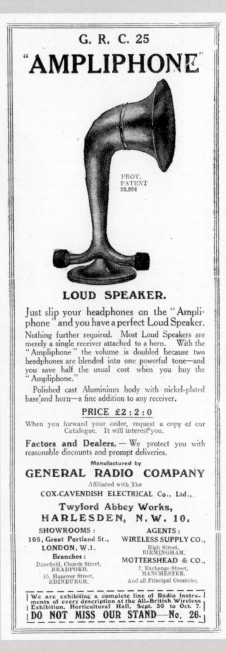

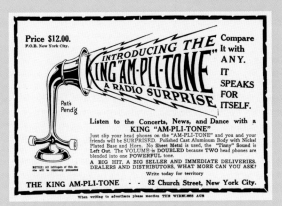

Wireless Age, May 1922.

Courtesy of John Jenkins.

Popular Wireless Weekly, September 30, 1922.

Courtesy of Martyn Bennett.

The G.R.C.27 Loudspeaker

The General Radio *G.R.C.27* loudspeaker of 1923 broke with conventional design in that the horn driver was contained in a French-polished mahogany cabinet. The cabinet design complemented the *G.R.C.16* receiver and *G.R.C.13* and *G.R.C.14* amplifiers. A graduated dial mounted on the front panel of the cabinet allowed mechanical adjustment of the driver to "*compensate for atmospheric variations.*" Priced at £7 10s. 0d. (£7.50), the *G.C.R.27* was considerably more expensive than competitive conventional horn speakers and it is doubtful whether it sold in any great numbers.

G.R.C. 29 Hearthside loudspeaker c. 1925.

G.R.C. 28 Pleasure Time loudspeaker c. 1925.

This poster, originally in colour, was featured in the *The Wireless Trader* in February 1925 as an example of well-designed advertising material. The 'other speaker' is, of course, the Speaker of the British House of Commons.

Note the artistic license used in foreshortening the horn to fit the confines of the advertisement.

Full Size Results – Half Price Cost

General Radio's straight-necked style horn speakers were very much in the North American style. More common among British manufacturers at the time was the curved 'swan-neck' style.

"HEARTHSIDE"
(Trade Mark Registered)
LOUD SPEAKER

The new General Radio " Hearthside " Loud Speaker gives full size results at half size cost. The secret of the full crystal clear volume is found in the new patented **cast-in diaphragm.**

A new and unique adjustment feature provides full adjustment control of the diaphragm and prevents any possibility of inferior results through overloading by powerful sets.

A point of great interest to those intent on perfect, distortionless reproduction is the fact that this new Loud Speaker is provided with a horn which is constructed entirely of a non-metallic substance, thus eliminating all vibration.

The superiority of the " Hearthside " is particularly evident on comparison test. The equal reproduction over an unusually wide scale is a revelation.

The " Hearthside " Loud Speaker is finished in crystalline black and will not look out of place in any room. Each instrument is carefully packed and fully guaranteed.

" It is altogether a well-made loud speaker, and worthy of the name of G.R.C."
— *" Broadcaster."*

35/-
Code Word : "HEARTHSIDE."
Type 29

FULL SIZE RESULTS—HALF SIZE COST

"PLEASURE TIME"
(Trade Mark Registered)
LOUD SPEAKER

The new General Radio " Pleasure Time " Loud Speaker has, in a remarkably short time, won for itself an enviable reputation for quality of reproduction unrivalled.

We reproduce here one or two of the many enthusiastic commendations accorded by Press and Public alike. The ultimate user is always the best judge.

The " Pleasure Time " is a " full size " Loud Speaker, which provides " full size " volume with a clarity and " natural " reproduction hitherto unknown. In the sensitive unit of the " Pleasure Time " are incorporated magnets and diaphragm of generous dimensions and a convenient adjustment Control Lever is provided. The terminals are polarity indicating.

Finished in crystalline black. Each instrument carefully packed in special container.

" We tested your ' Pleasure Time ' Loud Speaker against three other well-known makes and the result was overwhelmingly in favour of yours.
" If Loud Speakers were compared before purchase, we could not sell any other."
— *Radio Dealer.*
" Our test was carried out on a two-valve set of no particular merit, on which the valves were well past their prime ; but the 'Pleasure Time' played up magnificently, and many radio enthusiasts who instal the instrument will repeat the set-owner's gratified comment—that he had never heard a real loudspeaker before."
" British Trade Review."

70/-
Code Word : "PLEASTIME."
Type 28A

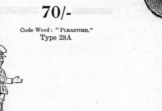

THE PERFECT REPRODUCER WITH THE NEW PATENT HORN

General Radio Company Catalogue, 1926.

The "Aristocrat" Loudspeaker

The 1925 General Radio Aristocrat loudspeaker, measuring 15 x 9 x 9 inches, employed an enclosed folded-horn some three feet in length. Housed in a hand-polished, dark walnut cabinet "of dignified design", the speaker was advertised to incorporate several patented features. No applicable patents, however, seem to have been issued to General Radio Company. Coming at a time when manufacturers were moving away from horn-style speakers to more efficient and better sounding enclosed, moving coil types – the Aristocrat was a last ditch effort to extend the appeal of the older technology.

G.R.C. Quality + Reasonable Price assure Increasing Sales

Wireless Components and Constructors' Sets

From its formation, General Radio Company's strategy included the design, manufacture and supply of a comprehensive range of components for both the amateur constructor and the smaller, independent wireless manufacturers. Innovation was key and in its later years the Company was issued with patents that included an improved valve-holder and headphone jack[18,19].

The component range included variometers, condensers, transformers, filament rheostats, jack plugs and sockets – in fact just about everything needed to build a complete receiver, with the exception of the valves. Even the interconnections could be made using G.R.C. bus-bar! The component business was evidently successful during the amateur construction boom years of 1923 and 1924. The low-frequency transformer (G.R.C.83) – the transformer which never fails – was particularly widely advertised and was reported in the trade press to sell extremely well. A compact wooden frame aerial (G.R.C.104), wound with some 160 feet of silk covered wire was offered for use with the company's valve receivers. In later years, high-tension batteries were available from the General Radio subsidiary, Radiobats.

The company's variometer (G.R.C.71) and vario-coupler (G.R.C.72) were highly regarded for their sensitivity. Notably, the stator and rotor coils were wound without supporting formers. According to the company literature, the coils were wound in an insulating solution that became "glass-hard" and held them rigidly in shape. The whole assembly was secured by an external aluminium cage, which allowed minimum separation between the coils and provided a degree of screening. Mercury contacts were used to reduce noise and eliminate wear during use. The device was given a special mention in the industry 'bible' – Harmsworth's Wireless Encyclopedia - and was used in that journal's design for a regenerative three-valve receiver. Advertisements for the variometer included a letter from the National Physical Laboratory attesting to its efficiency.

However, at £1 2s. 6d. the G.R.C.71 variometer was almost twice the price of competitive units on the market in 1923. It is doubtful whether very many budget conscious amateur constructors could have afforded such an outlay for their crystal sets – by far the biggest market at that time. By early 1924, in the face of both domestic and increasing foreign competition, the price was reduced to 15/-, but it was still one of the industry's most expensive components of its type. Following this price reduction, the Company announced in the February 1924 issue of Modern Wireless that it was now "making more variometers than any other manufacturer". Although sales no doubt increased, it is unlikely that this statement was entirely accurate.

Plans and explanatory notes describing receiver construction for the amateur wireless enthusiast could be obtained directly from the company or from any of its authorized dealers. The designs, of course, specified the use of General Radio components throughout. The impressively named 'General Radio Audiorad Reflex' receiver of 1923 was a particularly well-advertised design. Claimed by its designer to be the "most powerful single-valve circuit known", it was in fact a fairly standard reflex circuit by the standards of the day. Nevertheless, the design received favourable reviews in the wireless press and must have helped to boost overall sales of the Company's components.

As much as anything, it was perhaps the range of goods – from simple plugs and sockets to sophisticated drawing-room cabinet receivers – that stood General Radio apart from the other wireless manufacturers. It would be difficult to name another company that could have competed over such a broad array of products, although ironically it may well have been that the financial strain of managing this diversity contributed to General Radio's downfall.

The G.R.C. Audiorad Reflex Circuit

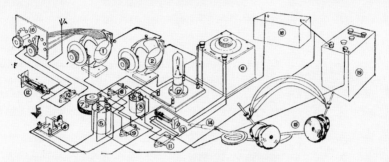

LOUD SPEAKER RESULTS WITH SINGLE VALVE!

1	G.R.C.72.	Vario-Coupler.	11	G.R.C.65.	Condenser.
2	G.R.C.71.	Variometer.	12	G.R.C.116.	Jack-Switch.
3	G.R.C.82.	Radioformer.	13	G.R.C.113.	Radiophone Jack.
4	G.R.C.123.	Crystal Detector.	14	G.R.C.111.	Radiophone Plug.
5	G.R.C.83.	Audioformer.	15	G.R.C.22.	Headphones.
6	G.R.C.62B.	Condenser.	16	Tap-Switch.	
7	G.R.C.92.	Radiostat.	17	Valve.	
8	G.R.C.65.	Condenser.	18	H.T. Battery.	
9	G.R.C.65.	Condenser.	19	L.T. Accumulator.	
10	G.R.C.65.	Condenser.			

G.R.C. Bus-bar wire used throughout.

"The one valve employed does double duty, amplifying at both radio and audio frequency. The construction of this set is easy and the operation simple. Especially noteworthy qualities of the circuit, aside from its amazing range and power, are the purity and clarity of reproduction, and the selective tuning.

Modern Wireless, September 1923.

G. R. C. 83		AUDIOFORMER.
G. R. C. 92		RADIOSTAT.

The G.R.C. Tuning Condenser – Years Ahead?

The new patented GENERAL RADIO Variable Condenser is years ahead of any variable condenser at present on the market – any Radio Engineer can see that by looking at it.

The *G.R.C.6* crystal receiver employed the company's own unusual variable tuning condenser. The condenser was a surface-mount design, in which the mechanism was contained entirely within the dial assembly. It was also used on the later *Unit-System* and *Type 15* and *Type 17* valve receivers.

The advantage was that it took up no space behind the panel. In practice, however, it was a rather cumbersome device. The mechanism was stiff to turn and, while the tuning range was admittedly large, it required two revolutions of the dial to cover the complete range. A harsh assessment might be that it was a "*solution looking for a problem.*"

Offered as a stand-alone component, it does not seem to have been used by other manufacturers and is rarely found on existing examples of amateur-built sets.

Although a patent application was apparently filed for the design, it was either abandoned or was rejected by the patent office as no known patent exists.

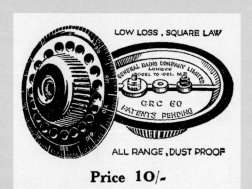

The Wireless World and Radio Review, October 21, 1925; November 4, 1925.

G.R.C. Components

REVIEW of APPARATUS

Latest Products of the Manufacturers.

GENERAL RADIO TELEPHONE TAGS.

To make provision for connecting a number of pairs of telephones either in series or parallel to a single pair of telephone terminals the General Radio Co., Ltd., 235, Regent Street, London, W.1,

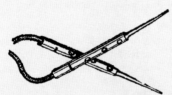

The General Radio Co.'s telephone tags permit of connecting several pairs of telephones either in series or parallel to a single pair of terminals.

have produced a tapering tag fitted with several holes into which the tags of other pairs of telephones can be plugged. Series and parallel connections can thus be obtained.

o o o o

The Wireless World and Radio Review, December 30th, 1925.

No detail of wireless apparatus or construction was apparently overlooked at General Radio. The company produced a comprehensive range of components for the amateur constructor.

For a company that produced receivers costing as much as a small car, it is all the more remarkable that they should have offered up such mundane items as these 'telephone tags'.

Right: *The Wireless Constructor*, May 1925.

Variometers and Vario-Couplers

The original 'wound-on-air' inductance

The General Radio Company tuning variometer and vario-coupler were constructed such that the coils were supported by an external, pressed aluminium, earthed cage allowing them to move within close proximity to each other – about 1/16 inch. Coil formers were dispensed with. This arrangement permitted improved stability and was supposed to offer better tuning sensitivity. Mercury contacts, were designed to eliminate scratching and noise and to resist wear. Although covered by a provisional patent number, no issued patent apparently exists.

"The General" appeared on all of General Radio Company's products, even components like this variometer where he was stamped into the metal support.

G. R. C. 71   VARIOMETER.
Prov. Pat. No. 409/23.

G. R. C. 72   VARIO-COUPLER.
Prov. Pat. No. 409/23.

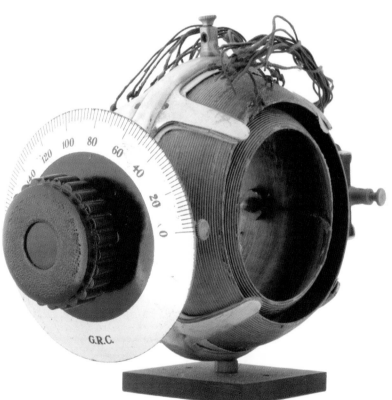

The G.R.C. variometer and vario-coupler (shown here) were supplied with the company's trademark nickel-plated brass dial and control knob. The primary (outer) winding of the vario-coupler was tapped in tens and units of turns, but was otherwise similar in mechanical construction to the variometer. The company initials printed on the dial often causes confusion in attributing amateur-built receivers and other manufacturer's products to General Radio Company.

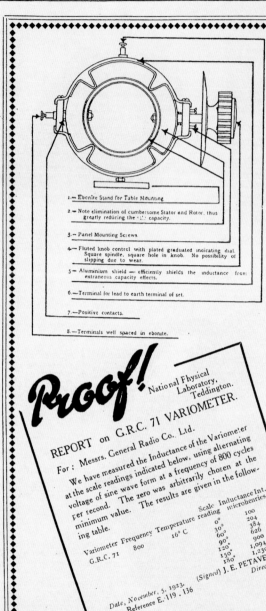
The Wireless Trader, January 1924.

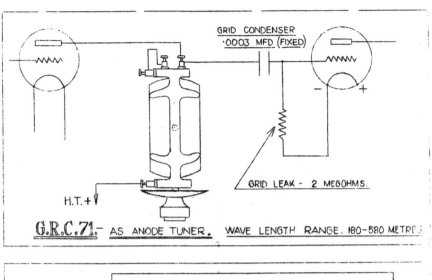

GRID CONDENSER
·0003 MFD (FIXED)

H.T.+

GRID LEAK - 2 MEGOHMS.

G.R.C. 71. - AS ANODE TUNER. WAVE LENGTH RANGE. 180-580 METRES

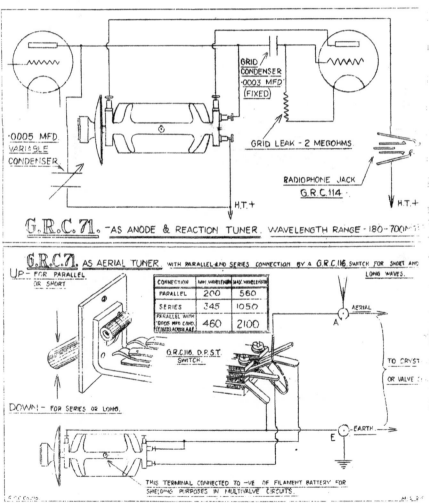

·0005 MFD.
VARIABLE
CONDENSER.

GRID
CONDENSER
·0003 MFD
(FIXED)

GRID LEAK - 2 MEGOHMS.

RADIOPHONE JACK
G.R.C. 114

H.T.+

H.T.+

G.R.C. 71. - AS ANODE & REACTION TUNER. WAVELENGTH RANGE - 180-700M

G.R.C. 71. AS AERIAL TUNER. WITH PARALLEL AND SERIES CONNECTION BY A G.R.C. 116. SWITCH FOR SHORT AND
LONG WAVES.

UP - FOR PARALLEL
OR SHORT

CONNECTION	MIN. WAVELENGTH	MAX. WAVELENGTH
PARALLEL	200	560
SERIES	345	1050
PARALLEL WITH ·0005 MFD COND. (FIXED) ACROSS A&E	460	2100

G.R.C. 116. D.P.S.T.
SWITCH.

AERIAL
A

TO CRYST
OR VALVE

DOWN - FOR SERIES OR LONG.

EARTH
E

THIS TERMINAL CONNECTED TO -VE OF FILAMENT BATTERY FOR
SHIELDING PURPOSES IN MULTIVALVE CIRCUITS.

The G.R.C. variometer and vario-coupler were supplied with comprehensive mechanical drawings and circuit connection particulars – typical of the thoroughness that was the hallmark of General Radio Company. A testimonial to the professional approach that the company took with every aspect of its business, such attention to detail was only matched by a few companies of the time.

Harmsworth's Three-Valve Regenerative Receiving Set

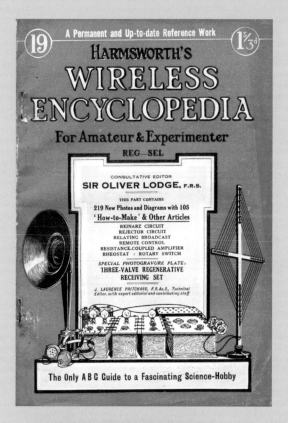

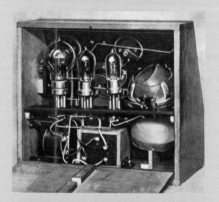

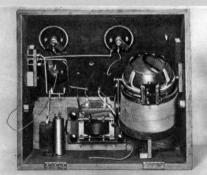

In July 1924, *Harmsworth's Wireless Encyclopedia* published construction plans for a three-valve regenerative receiver. The design involved a General Radio variometer fitted into a separate coil to provide the necessary reaction. The characteristic G.R.C. metal tuning dial can be seen in the above photograph, at lower left of the front panel.

In a later edition of the encyclopedia in a section dealing with variometers, the G.R.C. component was highlighted as an example of good design.

Leaders in Publicity

General Radio maintained an unusually active and, by inference, costly publicity department. The Company was ahead of its time with the adoption of a strategy of blanket media coverage and whilst its self-styled leadership in technology was open to debate, its leadership in marketing was not.

More typical of the practice in William Stephenson's native North America than in the British wireless industry, the Company continuously refreshed the appearance of its advertisements. Aware of the importance of targeting very specific audiences, the advertising copy for a given product would generally incorporate subtle variations in different journals. Advertisements for the same item in the same month would often be rewritten for a particular magazine. Most other wireless companies of the day, even the larger ones, routinely used the same copy.

General Radio advertised its products in just about every wireless journal and was frequently featured on the cover of the industry's leading trade mouthpiece – *The Wireless Trader*. Deservedly, the General Radio publicity department regularly received kudos from the technical press for the quality of the Company's catalogues and promotional literature.

G.R.C. Advertising — reaches every Radioist

Never the same advertisement twice!

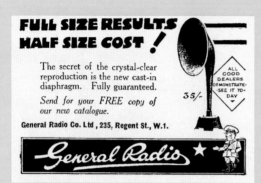

February 10, 1926.

February 17, 1926.

February 24, 1926.

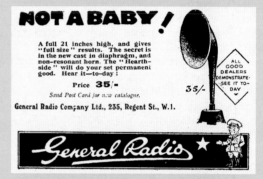

March 17, 1926.

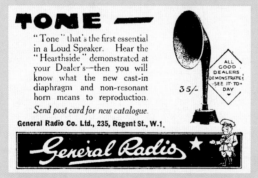

March 31, 1926.

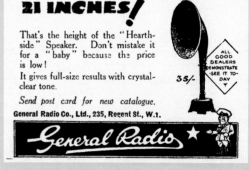

April 7, 1926.

Never the same advertisement twice? Well, almost. These advertisements appearing in *The Wireless World and Radio Review* in the first months of 1926 give an idea of the effort that the General Radio Company marketing department put into their material to ensure that the Company's advertisements were always fresh.

Modern Wireless, June 1925.

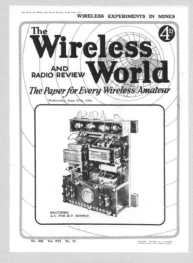

The Wireless World and Radio Review, June 17, 1925.

Expert Catalogue Work

Copy-writer, artist, lay-out man and printer are all to be congratulated on the General Radio Company's latest catalogue. One of the best points is the serious "reason why" attitude adopted in describing each line – one which cannot fail to carry conviction. Two-colour printing on a tinted paper gives the production a bright and colourful effect, unlike many wireless catalogues which, it will be agreed, are often far from "bright". Each page, too, has a most readable appearance – due, again, to skilful layout.

The Wireless Trader, October 28, 1925.

"Designed by the Publicity Department of the General Radio Company."

The Wireless Trader, February 18, 1925.

A Radiophone in Every Home.

The installation illustrated is just one of many types of G.R.C. Radio-phones. An ideal set for general use. Highly sensitive—selective and efficient—easy to operate—finely made in every detail. Meets the requirements of keen radioists who recognise and demand the best. Yet it is so simple to use that perfect results can readily be obtained by novices.

To the G.R.C.16 has been attached G.R.C.13 Amplifier and G.R.C.27 Loud Speaker. Connected to G.R.C.104 Frame Aerial, it obviates the necessity of erecting an outdoor aerial. With an outdoor aerial the minimum effective range on Loud Speaker is 100 miles.

G.R.C. RECEIVING EQUIPMENT is distributed only through the recognised Trade channels. In all respects it represents a sound selling proposition. Particulars should be in the hands of every progressive Dealer. G.R.C. "Dealers' Service Dept." is at your disposal.

The Wireless Trader, April 1923.

Appendix I.
General Radio Company Receiving Apparatus, 1922-1927

Model	Type	GPO No.	Price*	Year
G.R.C.	Crystal Receiver	n/a	-	1922 ?
G.R.C.2	Crystal Receiver	n/a	£6 6s. 0d.†	1922
G.R.C.11	Long-Range Tuner	n/a	-	1922
G.R.C.12	Detector-Capacity Unit	n/a	-	1922
G.R.C.4	Crystal Receiver	132	£3 8s. 0d.	1923
G.R.C.5	Crystal Receiver	140, 142	£1 18s. 0d.	
			£4 5s. 0d.†	1923
The Rex	Crystal Receiver	142	-	1923
G.R.C.13	Two-Valve LF Amplifier	3012	£11 10s. 0d.	1923
G.R.C.14	Three-Valve LF Amplifier		£15 10s. 0d.	1923
G.R.C.16	Two-Valve Receiver	2030	£14 5s 0d.	1923
G.R.C.17	Three-Valve Receiver	-	-	1923
G.R.C.18	One-Valve Receiver	-	£6 6s. 0d.†	1923
G.R.C.41	Four-Valve Portable	-	£48 15s. 0d.	1923
G.R.C.52	Four-Valve Cabinet Model	-	£49 7s. 0d	1923
G.R.C.55	Five-Valve Portable	-	-	1923
G.R.C.56	Five-Valve Cabinet Model	-	£70 15s. 0d.	1923
G.R.C.57	Five-Valve Cabinet Model	-	£90 5s. 0d.	1923
G.R.C.58	Six-Valve Cabinet Model	-	£169 15s. 0d.	1923
G.R.C.6	Crystal	-	£2 10s. 0d.	1924
G.R.C.501	One-Valve Receiver	n/a	£9 0s. 0d.	1925
G.R.C.502	One-Valve HF Amplifler	n/a	£6 0s. 0d.	1925
G.R.C.503	One-Valve LF Amplifier	n/a	£6 0s. 0d.	1925
G.R.C.504	One-Valve Power Amplifier	n/a	£7 0s. 0d.	1925
Type 15	Two-Valve Receiver	n/a	£12 0s. 0d. ††	1926
Type 17	Three-Valve Receiver	n/a	£15 0s. 0d. ††	1926
Model 2V	Two-Valve Receiver	n/a	£12 0s. 0d. ††	1927
Model 3V	Three-Valve Receiver	n/a	£15 0s. 0d. ††	1927

*   Earliest known advertised retail price; prices were reduced substantially over time.
†   With headphones and accessories
†† With loudspeaker, headphones, batteries, and accessories

Appendix II.
The British Broadcasting Company and Post Office Approval

Between 1923 and 1926 firms wishing to sell domestic broadcast receivers were obliged to become members of the British Broadcasting Company in order to be eligible to obtain the mandatory BBC stamp for their apparatus[17]. Along with BBC membership, approval to sell receivers required sanction from the Post Office Engineering Department and the issuing of a 'Type Approved Registration Number'.

General Radio was among the first group of companies to subscribe to the BBC, taking out ten shares (before the limited company was registered) and appears in the BBC's first shareholder return filed in March 1923.

Post Office registration procedures for wireless apparatus were in effect between and November 1st, 1922 and July 1st, 1924. In order for a manufacturer to obtain permission to sell equipment to the public, the regulations required a model of any new wireless receiver be submitted to the Post Office's Engineering Department for approval. The primary justification for such testing was to establish that valve receivers employing reaction would not cause interference arising from oscillations set up in the receiving aerial. While such a situation could not occur in crystal sets, they were, nevertheless, subjected to testing and approval. Manufacturers objected to the unnecessary bureaucracy, but were forced to comply. Later editions of the regulations stated that the object was to ensure that crystal receivers adequately covered the broadcast band – 350-425 metres, the wavelengths used by BBC stations. Ironically, the Post Office approval had no bearing on either the quality or performance of the set under test.

Much has been written on the vagaries of the Post Office registration and approval scheme[21] and will not be repeated here, other than to point out that the G.R.C.5 and The "Rex" crystal receivers illustrate some of the confusion and complexity that the scheme engendered. Two virtually identical versions of the G.R.C.5 set – the only electrical difference being the inclusion of a condenser across the headphone terminals (a minor change which, in any case, was standard practice at the time) – required that the sets be individually approved, with the corresponding issue of two different registration numbers (140 and 142) from the Post Office. On the other hand, a completely different model, The "Rex", could share the same registration number as one of the G.R.C.5 versions because the circuit was essentially the same.

Other than the G.R.C.16 and G.R.C.13 receiver and amplifier bearing the Post Office registration numbers 2030 and 3012, respectively no other numbers are known. The cabinet and portable receivers introduced in 1923 would certainly have required Post Office approval, but surprisingly no records have thus far been located.

Early General Radio receivers carried post office approval number stamped onto a metal plate fixed to the cabinet.

General Electric Co. Ltd.		Magnet House, Kingsway, London, W.C.2.	Electrical Apparatus Manufacturers		Two thousand, five hundred
General Radio Co.		Twyford Abbey Works, Harlesden, London, N.W.10			Ten
Gent	Bros.	49 Myddleton St, Clerkenwell, London, E.C.1.			Ten

Original entry showing General Radio Company had subscribed to ten shares in the first BBC return dated 16 March, 1923.

Conditions which Broadcast Receivers should fulfil
to obtain Post Office approval.
----

1. That all types of Broadcast Receivers may be constructed for
the reception of signals of any wavelengths.
2. That the apparatus shall be so constructed that it is
difficult to change the arrangement of the circuits
embodied in the design by means of external connections.
3. The following units, each of which must consist of apparatus
assembled connected and mounted in a single container, shall
be approved.
   a. Combined Tuner and Rectifier.
   b. Combined Tuner, High frequency amplifier and Rectifier.
   c. Audio Frequency Amplifier (of Valve or other type).
      Any combination of two or three of the above separate
      units (a) (b) & (c) will be allowed.
4. No receiving apparatus for general broadcast purposes shall
contain a valve or valves so connected as to be capable of
causing the aerial to oscillate.
5. Where reaction is used on to the first receiving circuit it
must not be adjustable but must be fixed and incapable of
causing oscillation.
6. Where reaction is used between a second or subsequent valve
on to the Anode Circuit of a valve connected to the aerial,
and there is no specific coupling provided between the first
receiving circuit and the first anode circuit the reaction
may be adjustable.
7. Tests of sets will be made on two aerials, one 30 ft.long
and the other 100 ft.long.
8. The sets will be tested for the production of oscillations
in the aerial and for interference properties with a factor
of safety, i.e.increasing the High Tension battery by about
30% changing valves, etc., but not by altering any soldered
connections.
9. The Postmaster General must be satisfied that sets containing
reaction can be reasonably repeated with consistent conditions.
10. After approval the type will be given a Post Office registered
number and makers must see that the sets fulfil the non
interfering conditions before they are sold. All sets sold
under the Broadcast licence shall bear the registered trade
mark of the Broadcasting Company and the Post Office
registered number.
11. The unit or set approved as the pattern instrument of a type
shall be retained without alteration by the maker. The
Postmaster General shall have the right at any time to select
any set of an approved type for test to see that the set is
reasonably similar to the approved pattern. In the case of
sets of an approved type employing reaction being found to
oscillate the aerial the Post Office may cancel the
authorisation of the future sale of that type. No change in
the design of any set or unit may be made after approval
without the previous sanction of the Postmaster General.

NOTE.

    The approval of the Postmaster General does not carry
any implied guarantee of the quality, workmanship or sensitivity of the apparatus.

                    Engineer-in-Chief's Office,
                      Wireless Section,
                        G.P.O. (West),
                          London, E.C.1.

Original proof of an early version of the Post Office registration conditions, dated October 1922. The relevant section dealing with changes to the registered design of equipment submitted for approval is outlined. At this stage, changes were still being made to the precise wording of the regulations, but they remained largely unchanged until the registration scheme was abandoned on July 1, 1924.

Appendix III.
The Cox-Cavendish Electrical Company

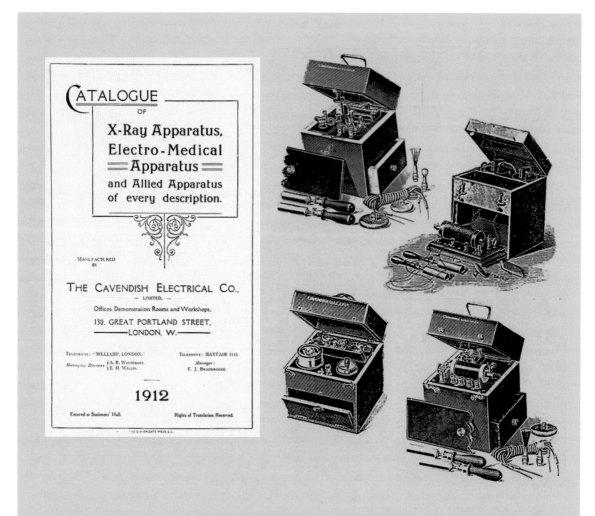

The Cox-Cavendish Electrical Company was formed in 1919 by the amalgamation of the Cavendish Electrical Company and Harry W. Cox & Company. Both were established companies in the medical equipment field engaged in the design and manufacture of electro-medical apparatus. This included the manufacture of so-called *Faradic Batteries and Coils*, often referred to as 'electric shock' machines, production of which continued after the two companies merged. These frightening devices were widely used at the time by physicians to deliver electrical impulses to patients as a cure for a variety of ailments, from nervous disorders and skin disease to stomach disorders.

Experiencing financial difficulties in the early 1920s, Cox-Cavendish dabbled with development of wireless apparatus as a potential new business opportunity. Notwithstanding the efficacy of the shock treatment, the design of the instruments themselves, consisting of coils, switches and brass or nickel-plated fittings meant that it should have been a relatively small step for the Company to construct wireless receivers.

The British Medical Journal, April 28th, 1923.

The demonstration rooms and offices of the Cavendish Electrical Company in Great Portland Street, London, ca.1912.

The early General Radio Company receivers carried the Cox-Cavendish affiliation acknowledgement on the cabinet.

William Stephenson, on his return to England after the war, appears to have invested in both General Radio and the Cox-Cavendish Electrical Company just at the time the latter was developing an interest in the domestic wireless market. His intention seems to have been to couple Cox-Cavendish's extensive experience in manufacturing high quality scientific apparatus with an existing domestic wireless enterprise. So in 1922, under Stephenson's influence, General Radio contracted with Cox-Cavendish to manufacture wireless receivers. These original General Radio Company wireless products are distinguished by the marking clearly showing the affiliation with Cox-Cavendish.

The Cox-Cavendish Electrical Company was liquidated in May 1924. Production of electro-medical equipment continued under the name of Stanley Cox Limited, but Stephenson's involvement with the company ended.

Example of a particularly well constructed Cox-Cavendish
electric shock apparatus.

This instrument, with a hinged mahogany panel and lacquered brass fittings, is another example of Cox-Cavendish workmanship.

The *Eros Faradic Battery* appeared in the 1912 Cox-Cavendish Electro-Medical Apparatus Catalogue, priced at £1 18s. 0d. (£1.90). A three position on-off switch enabled the coil to be worked with either one dry-cell battery for *'weaker currents'* or with two cells when *'very strong currents'* were needed. Regulation of the current was effected by sliding a nickel-plated tube in and out of the cylindrical coil.

Cox-Cavendish – Contract Manufacturing

The Cox-Cavendish Electrical Company is known to have manufactured wireless equipment for other companies. This 1922 portable receiver, designed by Reginald Charles Clinker of the British Thomson-Houston Company of Rugby, carries a label indicating that the set, serial number R241, was built at the Cox-Cavendish factory in Harlesden. A further example, bearing the serial number R112 (see image of label plate shown bottom left), is held in the Science Museum reserve collection store in London.

Cox-Cavendish was engaged in the contract manufacturing business at around the time that William Stephenson purchased an interest in both the Cox-Cavendish and General Radio Companies. It is not clear whether he was involved in the decision for the company to contract manufacture or indeed if he even supported the activity. It is quite possible that with the collaboration with General Radio in place, Stephenson would have preferred not to provide support for competitors like British Thomson-Houston. In any event, given the large number of British Thomson-Houston receivers that have survived and the rarity of the Cox-Cavendish identification, it is likely that this was not a long-term relationship. BTH's reputation, however, for producing high-quality wireless products in the early 1920s speaks well of Cox-Cavendish's manufacturing capabilities.

PORTABLE WIRELESS RECEIVER.

This Receiver is unique due to the fact that it has a very large range of operation without attachment to any external or earth wires. Its operation is extremely simple and does not require any technical knowledge of wireless science or electrical engineering.

The whole apparatus is contained in a compact and highly finished cabinet. It acts both as a receiver, direction finder and wave meter. It is suitable for either continuous wave, spark gap or tonic train telegraphy, or (when connected to a small external wire) wireless telephony and wireless music.

It is easily portable, weighing only 18 lb. complete.

It has many applications and is adaptable for use with a large number of accessories such as :—

> One-, two- or three-valve low frequency amplifiers.
>
> Loud speaker equipment.
>
> Inker equipment for recording the Morse Code on tape.

Full prices and particulars quoted on application.

———

THE BRITISH THOMSON-HOUSTON CO., LTD.,
RUGBY, ENGLAND.

MARCH, 1922.   AG 134

The BTH Portable Wireless Receiver was manufactured by Cox-Cavendish at the Harlesdon factory. The extent of the relationship between the two companies or whether other models were built by Cox-Cavendish is not known.

THE COX-CAVENDISH ELECTRICAL COMPANY,
LIMITED.

Board of Directors.

A. MORPHY, O.B.E., *Chairman.*
F. WISSLER. *Vice-Chairman.*
H. E. DONNITHORNÉ, A.M.I.E.E.
E. H. WILLIS.
B. H. MORPHY, M.I.E.E.
W. S. STEPHENSON.

Bankers.

WESTMINSTER BANK, LIMITED.

Auditors.

EDWARD MOORE & SONS, Chartered Accountants, Thames House, Queen Street Place, E.C.4.

Board of Directors.

A. MORPHY, O.B.E., *Chairman.*
F. WISSLER. *Vice-Chairman.*
H. E. DONNITHORNÉ, A.M.I.E.E.
E. H. WILLIS.
B. H. MORPHY, M.I.E.E.
W. S. STEPHENSON.

Twelfth Report of the Directors of the Cox-Cavendish Electrical Company, Limited, on Accounts to 30th June, 1923.

The Directors beg to submit their Twelfth Report to the Shareholders, together with Balance Sheet at June 30th, 1923.

It will be observed that the accounting period has been extended to fifteen months, instead of twelve, owing to the dislocation of business that stocktaking would have entailed at March 31st, which would have seriously interfered with the production of the Company's manufactures for urgent contracts at a critical period.

The Profit and Loss Account for the same period will be laid before the Company at the General Meeting in accordance with the provisions of the Articles of Association.

Although the year's working shows a loss, your Directors following the dictates of sound policy have deemed it advisable to make adequate provision for Depreciation of Plant, Furniture, Fixtures, and various other items as set forth in the Balance Sheet, bringing the total loss on the trading for the period to £5,592 19s. 0d.

The Directors whilst regretting this loss, are glad it is very much less than for the preceding period, and would call attention to the greatly increased turnover shown in the accounts, as indicating substantial growth in the volume of business handled by the Company. They confidently anticipate, having regard to the large total value of outstanding orders now on the books, that the accounts for the current year will show a very different result.

The Directors regret that the anticipation of a revival in trade which appeared imminent at the date of the last Annual General Meeting, particularly in connection with the expected advent of Broadcasting Music, Speech, etc., by Wireless Telephony, did not materialise for some months later, owing to delays in effecting an agreement between the British Broadcasting Company (with which this Company is connected through its affiliated Company, as members) and the Postmaster General, and the loss incurred may be attributed entirely to this cause.

Advantage was taken, however, during this period to carry out a great amount of experimental and development work on the many types of Wireless Receiving Sets and Head Phones now so popular with the public, so that when the demand ultimately came the Company was able to cope with a considerable volume of business.

The last three months of the fiscal period under review produced the largest turnover of any similar period in the history of the Company, but the profits realised were not sufficient to make up the leeway for the preceding months.

In connection with the Experimental and Development work on Wireless Apparatus which involved very heavy expenditure owing to its special nature, and to the fact that it comprised about 75 per cent. of the total production at the Factory for apparatus of entirely new types, the Directors have carried forward as an asset in the Balance Sheet the minimum sum, which has been expended on this work, and in respect of which the Company will benefit in the coming years. This amount will be written off from time to time, as it was felt that to debit the whole cost to the present period would be unfair. As to the prospects of this new departure in the type of apparatus made by the Company, it is of course hardly necessary to repeat that in considered judgment of the world's leading statesmen, and thinkers in every department of life, Broadcasting has come to stay, and will prove a means of education and a source of delightful entertainment to millions of people all over the world. The science is essentially progressive and great developments are anticipated in the very near future.

Since the date of the last Meeting, the Company has entered into a very satisfactory Agreement with a leading firm supplying Wireless Telephony Instruments, for the manufacture of their products, and has received large contracts from them for this type of apparatus.

Further information will be furnished in reference to this Agreement at the Annual Meeting.

The Directors regret to report the death of Mr. A. R. Winterson, one of the former Managing Directors. They have elected Mr. W. S. Stephenson a Director of the Company, subject to confirmation at the forthcoming Meeting.

The Company's Auditors, Messrs. Edward Moore & Sons, retire, and are eligible for re-election.

By order of the Board,

E. H. WILLIS,
Secretary.

Report of the Directors of the Cox-Cavendish Electrical Company, dated June 30 1923 for the fifteen months beginning April 1, 1922 announcing William Stephenson's election to the board. The report also announces the agreement to manufacture Wireless Telephony Instruments for 'leading firm'.

Appendix IV.
A New Method of Television

This is a verbatim transcript of an article appearing in *Radio News*, April 6, 1925.

A New Method of Television.
by W. G. Walton.

Below is given a description of the newest method of transmitting photographs by radio or wire at such a speed as to enable the distant envisioning of transpiring events.

Mr. W. G. Walton, in the interest of scientific progress, has kindly given an interview for "Radio News" in which he explains the great difficulties in accomplishing the "Radio Movie," the ultimate object of his research. Both he and Mr. W. S. Stephenson, of the General Radio Company, London, have done a great deal of research work in the matter of the transmission of Pictures by radio, and have made some highly interesting discoveries.

What has been done.
"For a matter of 30 to 40 years attempts to transmit pictures by electrical means have been made, and the advent of the motion picture led to dreams of transmitting pictures at such a speed that a motion picture effect could be produced," Mr. Walton said.

"The light sensitive device has been, and still is, the greatest source of our troubles. Selenium cells have the disadvantage of slow action and lag, while photo-electric cells, though faster, give only very minute currents which need amplifying by many stages of resistance coupled vacuum tube amplifiers. Neither of these devices is a desirable feature of commercial apparatus. The time required by the fastest apparatus is too long. To be an entire success, apparatus must be faster and such that it can be used at a moment's notice without many adjustments, and the reception of a reasonable picture must be a certainty.

"Television or the radio movie," he continued, "is the transmission and reception of pictures by electricity in such rapid succession that a motion picture effect is obtained. Apparatus for this purpose is generally the same as that used in the transmission of photographs, but operating at a much greater speed."

One method.
One of the methods is to traverse the picture in lines by optical arrangements and transmitting impulses, the strength of which depends on the intensity of the small sections of these lines as they are shown in succession on a light sensitive device.

At the receiving end a beam of light varied in intensity by a shutter actuated by the impulses received from the transmitting end is traversed over a screen by an optical arrangement similar to that used at the transmitting end. Everything depends upon the rate at which the light sensitive device can respond and also the light controlled shutter at the receiving end. This refers to schemes using one cell.

Millions of dots.
Before difficulties in the way of television can he appreciated, the number of dots necessary to produce a reasonable picture must be known. Television to be a complete success must have almost as good a definition as the standard motion picture. With a picture of one square foot consisting of a million dots and held a foot away from the eye, an average person will be able to distinguish the dots. Such a picture will give good detail of a town or landscape view.

Speed.
Motion pictures are shown at the rate of 16 per second. Taking this as the rate at which complete pictures must be

The reproducing apparatus which recreates the image transmitted to it by the sender

repeated by television apparatus, our light sensitive device in single cell methods has to respond to 18,000,000 different impulses per second. and so must the light control shutters. This is, of course, putting the problem at its worst. Some investigators have stated that 300,000 (an enormous difference) will suffice. Allowing that the number of complete pictures is 10 per second, our picture consists of 30,000 dots, 150 lines of 200 dots each. Take any magazine or newspaper picture and mark off 30,000, the picture within this area can hardly be said to have good detail, certainly not in a landscape or incident picture.

We are striving to produce something as good as the motion picture, and though 18,000,000 per second is high, it is a good ideal to aim at. Light sensitive devices as used up to the present time have not been able to respond to anything like such a speed.

"Mr. W. S. Stephenson and I," Mr. Walton continued, "have done a considerable amount of research work. In an endeavor (sic) to discover something much faster, we tried the possibilities of vacuum tubes to see if light would affect a stream of electrons by bending the stream or otherwise producing some action. Results were doubtful, masked by other things such as light from the filaments.

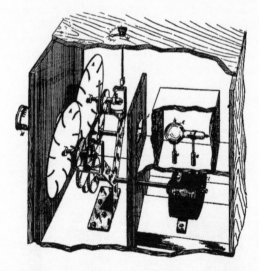

Above is a plan in perspective of the new television transmitter. Note the position of the lens, M, and the lightsensitive cell, K.

"Although we have not abandoned this idea, we are trying another line of investigation which shows great possibilities. We have hopes of producing a light sensitive arrangement with a reverse effect, so that an extremely rapid shutter will not be required at the receiving end."

Heterodyning wave-lengths.

Light waves are electromagnetic in nature, differing from radio waves only as regards wave-length, though the difference is great. Our endeavor (sic) is to convert light frequencies into radio frequencies by an action similar to heterodyning (superimposing one wave-length on another) in several steps. The radio frequency thus produced is, after amplification, transmitted direct without modulating a carrier wave. The possibility is now apparent. A picture consisting of light waves is converted into an invisible picture of radio waves which, after amplification and reconversion at the receiving end, produces a visible image on the screen. As just described, the trouble is in sorting out the waves and putting them in their respective positions at the receiving end. But if the picture at the sending end is split into sections, and each section has a frequency of its own, then the rearrangement at the receiving end is only a matter of reversing the operations which took place at the transmitter.

The transmission of the pictures would mean the use of a band of wavelengths, but, after all, radio telephony has the same difficulty. The speed of operation need not be considered with such an arrangement and natural colors mean little further complication.

The process used at present.

"I have explained," Mr. W. G. Walton told "Radio News," "the difficulty in breaking up the picture into dots at a sufficiently high speed to produce an illusion of motion. I will now tell you how Mr. Stephenson and myself tackle the problem with our apparatus. The method used is by causing apertures formed by the intersection of slots arranged around the periphery of two discs to traverse the picture. These discs may be rotated in the same or opposite directions, according to the number and disposition of slots used and the relative speeds of the two discs. In the sketches, the discs (A) are of the same diameter, have the same number of slots each, and rotate in the same direction. They are arranged to overlap about 1½ inches, consequently the slots of one disc are moving downward and the slots of the second disc upwards. As the slots of one disc are at an angle to those in the second, a minute aperture is formed at the point of intersection, which, when the discs are rotating, passes from one side to the other. Immediately one pair of slots has become disengaged, the next pair engage. Should the two discs be rotating at the same speed, all the apertures will follow the same path, a line, curved or straight, depending on the shape of the slots, from right to left. Now should one disc rotate a little faster than the other, each successive aperture will traverse a line a little above or below the line traversed by the last aperture.

"The effect of all this." continued Mr. Walton, "is equivalent to causing a pinhole to traverse an area in successive lines from right to left, each line just above the last, until the whole area has been covered, when the same process is repeated, starting at the bottom. The great advantages of this method are that there is no waste time, some part of the area is always covered by the pinhole, the pinhole is always open and not arranged for a series of rapid flashes, and lastly, speed of traverse is practically the same over the whole area.

The transmitter.

"The transmitting instrument is arranged somewhat similar to a camera," explained Mr. Walton. "A lens (M) (on the sketch) throws an inverted image about one inch square in a plane parallel to and just between the overlapping discs (A, A). The slots in the discs are about .002 of an inch wide, therefore the pinhole formed by intersecting slots is about the same diameter. As I explained, the pinhole traverses the whole of the inverted image, allowing a small area of light at a time to pass through. This light is then focussed by a lens marked (J) onto a light sensitive cell (K). The varying electric currents from the cell and a speed control current are then transmitted by radio or other means to the receiving station.

The receiving station.

"It is obvious that similar sets of discs must be used both at the transmitting and receiving stations," Mr. Walton continued. "At the receiving station a source of intense white light such as an electric arc is placed behind the lens marked (F), which concentrates the beam on a light control shutter (C), shown diagrammatically as a four-string Einthoven galvanometer. The light having been controlled by the shutter is then thrown on a white diffusing screen (B). An area of this screen throws light through the aperture formed by the slots of the discs onto the lens (H), which focusses (sic) the light in a spot on an ordinary projection screen. The received electric current, i. e., current corresponding to the current from the light sensitive cell at the transmitting end, and the speed control current, are applied, the first to the light control shutter (C), and the second to maintain synchronism between the transmitting and receiving machines.

"It is possible when the two machines have just been started and synchronized that the spot of light shown on the screen is not in its correct position, in which case by means of the 'advance' or 'retard control (I) can be rectified even while the machine is rotating at full speed.

"I have mentioned the spot of light shown on the screen, but actually this spot would be moving at such a speed that a continuous image would be seen much the same as the motion picture image.

Some remarkable figures.

"This is the type of machine which was evolved after careful consideration of many ways of accomplishing the results. Quite the most important point is the amount of light passing through the shutters onto the light sensitive cell, and at the receiving end tonto the screen. With the above method the focussing of the beam of light at the receiving end into a narrow pencil of light is unnecessary.

The amount of definition available is purely a question of the width of the slots and the gearing of the discs. We use slots .002 inch wide, and one disc does 1000 revolutions while the other does 999, consequently our picture consists of 1000 lines with 50 per cent overlap between lines. The number of dots in each line - if such a term may be used depends on the speed of the light sensitive cell and the light control shutter. Should the cell be slow, it will respond only to an average effect beyond its speed of response; in other words, the reproduction would be very blurred. These remarks apply also to the light control shutter.

Three-color method.

"Another interesting arrangement we have brought out is for natural color reproductions. This is a three-color method similar to that used in photography. At the transmitting end there are three light sensitive cells, each of which respond only to one color and at the receiving end there are three light control shutters, each actuated by currents from one light sensitive cell only. The shutters pass light only of one of the three colors which are mixed and then shown on the screen. The shutter in this case could be a three-string Einthoven, each string independently operated.

I hope,' concluded Mr. Walton, "that what I have told you will be of use to other experimenters along the same lines."-"Radio News," April, 1925.

Appendix V:
The *Filonator* – Technical Details

The *Filonator*, as General Radio christened the device in 1927, was a two-fluid 1½-volt primary cell. According to the Company's literature it could be *"recharged instantly in the listener's home simply by inserting special compressed tablets"* eliminating the need to carry heavy accumulators to a local charging station. The cell was the invention of the Belgian engineer, Leopold Darimont and was initially manufactured and distributed in the United Kingdom by Darimont Electric Batteries Limited of 329, High Holborn, London, W.C.1.

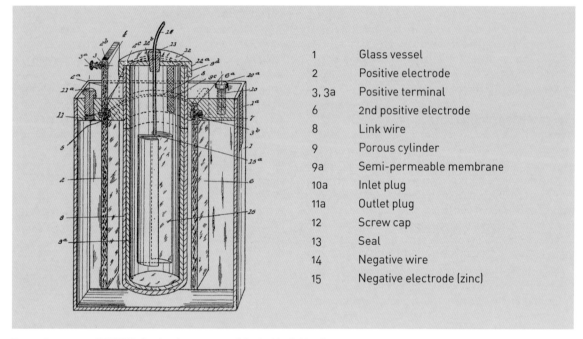

1	Glass vessel
2	Positive electrode
3, 3a	Positive terminal
6	2nd positive electrode
8	Link wire
9	Porous cylinder
9a	Semi-permeable membrane
10a	Inlet plug
11a	Outlet plug
12	Screw cap
13	Seal
14	Negative wire
15	Negative electrode (zinc)

Extract from patent GB241729 showing the structure of the double-fluid cell.

The *Filonator* consisted of a glass vessel containing one or more positive carbon electrodes and a negative zinc electrode housed in a porous cylinder filled with an 'exciter' solution. A depolarising solution surrounded the positive electrodes and was separated from the exciter solution by a semi-permeable membrane formed on the inner surface of the porous cylinder. The membrane was designed to prevent the two solutions actually mixing, but still allow the passage of ions between them.

The chemistry given in British patent GB241729 for the cell's solutions was diverse, but a typical formulation was:

Exciter solution:		**Depolarising solution:**	
		Perchloride of iron, Fe_2Cl_6	750g
Sodium chloride, NaCl	250g	Nitric acid, HNO_3	10cc
Zinc chloride, $ZnCl_2$	10g	with or without chromium trioxide, CrO_3	
Zinc sulphate , $ZnSO_4$	5g	or	
		Iron sulphate, $Fe_2(SO_4)_3$	500g
In sufficient water to optimize		Sulphuric acid, H_2SO_4	8cc
electric capacity.		In sufficient water to create a solution with the same concentration as the exciter solution.	

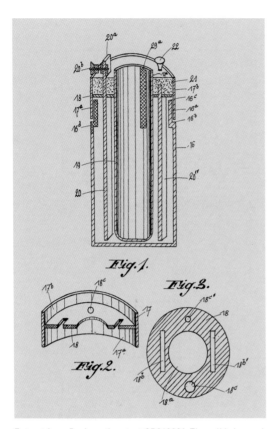

Extract from Darimont's patent GB263081. The cell is housed in a more compact cylindrical vessel and the design is generally more manufactureable.

Experience showed that the presence of salts in the exciter solution such as sodium- or potassium-chloride upset the osmotic balance of the cell. This resulted in the exciter solution combining with the depolarizing liquid, causing the cell to overflow with unfortunate consequences. Darimont addressed this serious problem in British patent GB250803 by modifying the semi-permeable membrane, claiming it prevented what he graphically described as a 'tedious sucking' of the liquid in the cell. The improvement was apparently not all Darimont had hoped for and a subsequent patent, GB266662, specified further improvements. It seems likely, however, that the problem of *tedious sucking* was never fully resolved.

The Darimont cell relied upon a complex mix of both organic and inorganic substances* and had to maintain a critical osmotic balance in order to avoid catastrophic spillages. In addition, the integrity of a number of fluid-tight seals was required throughout the life of the cell. It is a matter of speculation as to whether such a device could ever have been made reliable enough for the domestic wireless market; certainly there seems to be no surviving example of the *Filonator*.

*Among the myriad of components used by Darimont were wax, powdered coke, corn starch, soap, linseed oil, chalk, kaolin, caustic soda, dextrin, plus the exciter and depolarising chemicals, examples of which are cited above.

Appendix VI:
Circuit Diagrams

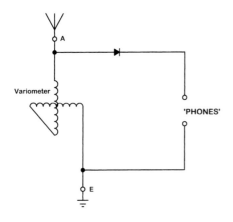

G.R.C. Crystal Receiver

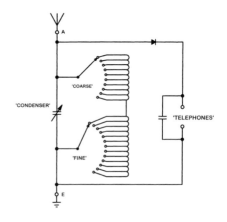

G.R.C.2 Crystal Receiver

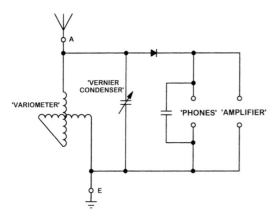

G.R.C.4 Crystal Receiver

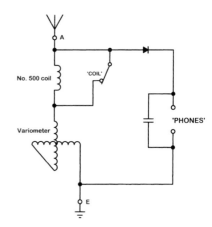

G.R.C.5 Crystal Receiver
(GPO No.140)

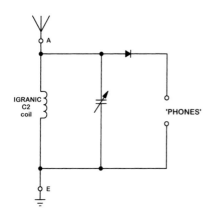

G.R.C.5 (GPO No.142) and The "Rex"

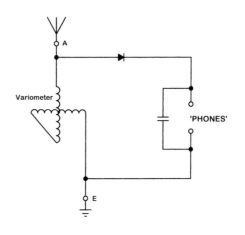

G.R.C.6 Crystal Receiver

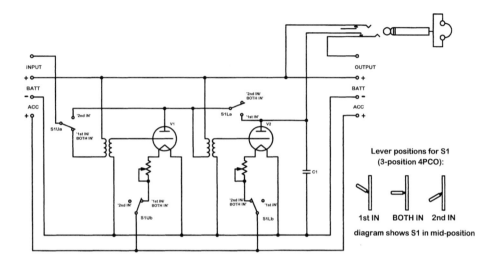

G.R.C.13 Two-Valve Amplifier

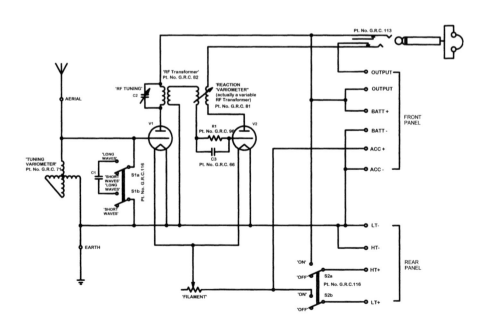

G.R.C.16 Two-Valve Receiver

Bibliographical References

1. Stevenson, William: *A Man Called Intrepid*. Published by The Lyons Press, Guilford, Connecticut, 1976.
2. Conant, Jennet: *The Irregulars: Roald Dahl and the British Spy Ring in Wartime Washington*.
    Published by Simon & Schuster, NY, New York, 2008.
3. Macdonald, Bill: *The True 'Intrepid' – Sir William Stephenson*. Published by Timberholme Books Ltd., Surrey,
    British Columbia, Canada, 1998.
4. Briggs, Asa: *The History of Broadcasting in the United Kingdom; Volume 1 – The Birth of Broadcasting*.
    Published by Oxford University Press, London, 1961.
5. Hyde, H. Montgomery: Room 3603 – *The Story of the British Intelligence Center in New York during World War II*.
    Published by Farrar, Straus and Company, NY, New York, 1962. Published in the UK (1962) by Hamish Hamilton,
    London as "*The Quiet Canadian: The Secret Service Story of Sir William Stephenson*".
6. *The Radio Year Book*. Sir Isaac Pitman & Sons Ltd., London, 1923, 1924.
7. Stephenson, William and Walton, George: *Improvements Relating to Telephone Instruments*. British Patent
    GB244170. Issued December 11, 1925.
8. Walters, Marylu: CKUA – *Radio Worth Fighting For*. Published by The University of Alberta Press, Edmonton,
    Alberta, Canada, 2002.
9. McArthur, Tom and Waddell, Peter: *The Secret Life of John Logie Baird*. Published by Hutchinson Ltd.,
    London, 1986.
10. Baker, T. Thorne: *The Telegraphic Transmission of Photographs*. Published by Constable &
    Company Limited, London, 1910.
11. Baker, T. Thorne: *Wireless Pictures and Television*. Published by Constable & Company Limited, London, 1926.
12. Black, Harry: *Canadian Scientists and Inventors*. Published by Pembroke Publishers Limited,
    Ontario, Canada, 2008.
13. Geddes, Keith and Bussey, Gordon: *The Setmakers – A History of the Radio and Television Industry*.
    Published by BREMA, London, 1991.
14 Walton, William George: *A New Method of Television*. Article appearing in Radio News, April 6, 1925.
15. Keay, Andrew, Boraine, Andre and Burdette, David: *Preferential Debts in*
    Corporate Insolvency: A Comparative Study. Published in International Insolvency Review, Vol. 10. John Wiley
    and Sons, 2001. This work cites Court Proceedings, Weekly Notes, June 22 1929 pages 172-173.
16. Walton, William George and General Radio Company: *Improvements in the Construction of Cabinets and*
    Framework of Wireless Receiving Sets. British Patent GB268475. Issued April 7, 1927.
17. Clark, Lorne: *Shareholders of the British Broadcasting Company*. Published by BVWS Books, 2010.
18. Walton, William George and General Radio Company: *Improvements Relating to Telephone Jacks and Jack*
    Switches Particularly for Use in Wireless Signaling Apparatus and Telephone Switching. British Patent GB274249.
    Issued July 21, 1927.
19. Walton, William George and General Radio Company: *Improvements Relating to Holders for Thermionic Valves*
    or Discharge Tubes. British Patent GB277101. Issued September 9, 1927.
20. Thrower, Keith: *British Radio Valves: The Classic Years 1926 –1946*. Published by Speedwell, UK, 2009.
21. Sanders, Ian L: *Tickling the Crystal – Domestic British Crystal Sets of the 1920s. (Volumes 1-5.)*
    Published by BVWS Books, 2001-2010.

General Bibliography

Bussey, Gordon: *Vintage Crystal Sets, 1922-1927*. Published by IPC Electrical-Electronic Press, London, 1976.

Bussey, Gordon: *Wireless, The Crucial Decade, 1924-34*.
Published by Peter Peregrinus Ltd., London, 1990, ISBN 0863411886.

Constable, Anthony: *Early Wireless*. Published by Midas Books, Kent, 1980, ISBN 085936125X.

Hill, Jonathan: *Radio! Radio!* Published by Sunrise Press, Bampton, Devon, 1996, ISBN 0951144871.

Hill, Jonathan: *The Cat's Whisker*. Published by Oresko Books Ltd., London, 1978, ISBN 0905368460.

Murray, Robert P, Editor: *The Early Development of Radio in Canada, 1901-1930*.
Published by Sonoran Publishing, LLC, Chandler, Arizona, USA, 2005, ISBN 188660620.

Image Sources and Credits

The following list shows sources and credits for images where specific permission to publish or specific source details were required.

Page	Image details	Source and Acknowledgment
vi	Flagship Apple Store, 235 Regent Street, London W1, in 2011.	Reproduced with the kind permission of Carl Glover.
xiv	Statue of Sir William Stephenson in his First World War aviator's uniform.	Reproduced with the kind permission of Pawan Singal.
5	Vigfus and Kristin Stephenson, 1912.	Reproduced with the kind permission of Bill Macdonald.
6	Extract, 1901 Canadian census, District 12 Winnipeg.	Library and Archives Canada.
6	Attestation papers from World War I Personnel Records of William Samuel Stephenson.	Library and Archives Canada/Ministry of the Overseas Military Forces of Canada fonds/Accession no. 1992-93/166/Box no. 9279-11.
7	Top, First World War ace – the young Captain Stephenson.	Reproduced with the kind permission of Bill Macdonald.
7	Bottom left, Stephenson (right) and comrades, Beauvois, 1919.	Reproduced with kind permission of the Trustees of the Royal Air Force Museum.
7	Bottom right, 'Stephenson (right) and comrade Baldwin, c1919.	Reproduced with kind permission of the Trustees of the Royal Air Force Museum.
8	Top left, Stephenson in Fedora hat.	Reproduced with the kind permission of Bill Macdonald.
8	Marriage certificate, William Stephenson and Mary Simmons.	Source: UK General Register Office, Crown copyright.
8	William Stephenson with his 6-valve cabinet receiver of 1922.	Reproduced with the kind permission of Bill Macdonald.
9	WWI Service Record, William Stephenson.	Source: National Archives file AIR 76/482, image 165. Reproduced with the kind permission of the National Archives, UK.
10	Passenger manifest, Canadian Pacific vessel Montcalm. 14 May 1922.	Reproduced with the kind permission of the National Archives, UK.
12	Top, Donal Morphy and Charles Richards.	Reproduced with the kind permission of Morphy-Richards Ltd.
12	Marmite Jar.	Unknown. Please contact the authors if you own the copyright for this photograph.
13	Royal Aero Club record, William Ewart Gladstone Murray.	www.ancestry.co.uk. Reproduced with the kind permission of the Royal Aero Club.
19	Extracts from patent GB218766.	Reproduced with the kind permission of the European Patents Office (EPO) whose website may be found at: http://www.epo.org/index.html Use of content from the EPO website is governed by Article 5 'Copyright, use of content' of the EPO Terms and Conditions which may be found at: http://www.epo.org/footer/terms.html#Copyright
21	Image of two skiers.	*The Daily Mail*, December 27, 1922. From a microfilm held by the British Library Newspaper Library, Colindale, UK.
23	Extract from patent GB190218.	Reproduced with the kind permission of the European Patents Office (EPO) whose website may be found at: http://www.epo.org/index.html Use of content from the EPO website is governed by Article 5 'Copyright, use of content' of the EPO Terms and Conditions which may be found at: http://www.epo.org/footer/terms.html#Copyright
38	Front cover of The Illustrated London News, May 15, 1926.	Source: http://www.iln.org.uk/ . Reproduced with the kind permission of John Weedy.
47	GRC crystal receiver.	Photograph by Ian Sanders.
48	G.R.C.2 crystal receiver.	Photograph courtesy of Robert Murray.

Page	Image details	Source and Acknowledgment
48	G.R.C.4 crystal receiver.	Photograph courtesy of Erwin Macho.
49	G.R.C.5 crystal receivers – P.O. Nos. Reg. 140 and 142.	Photographs by Carl Glover.
50	Rex crystal receiver.	Photograph by Carl Glover.
51	G.R.C.6 crystal receiver.	Photograph by Carl Glover.
55	G.R.C.16 two-valve receiver.	From the Mike Kempe collection. Photograph by Carl Glover, retouching by Lorne Clark.
55	G.R.C.13 two-valve amplifier.	Photograph by Lorne Clark.
63	G.R.C. Type 15 receiver.	Photograph courtesy of Steve Harris.
63	G.R.C. Type 17 receiver.	Photographs courtesy of Martin Francis.
64	Extract from patent GB268475.	Reproduced with the kind permission of the European Patents Office (EPO) whose website may be found at: http://www.epo.org/index.html Use of content from the EPO website is governed by Article 5 'Copyright, use of content' of the EPO Terms and Conditions which may be found at: http://www.epo.org/footer/terms.html#Copyright
67	Scanned images from 1926 G.R.C. advertising brochure.	Brochure from the Gordon Bussey collection, scans by Robert Mance.
69	Photograph of G.R.C. 3-valve receiver of 1927.	From the original negative of Fig. 223, p88, Radio!Radio!, Sunrise Press, 1986, ISBN0951144871; courtesy of Jonathan Hill. Retouching by Lorne Clark.
70	Drawing of 0-V-2 General Radio receiver.	This excellent drawing by Norman Jackson appeared in the Bulletin of the British Vintage Wireless Society, May 1982. Reproduced with the kind permission of the British Vintage Wireless Society.
71	Radiobats entry in the list of shareholders of the British Broadcasting Company.	Source: National Archives file BT 31/27633/186424. Reproduced with the kind permission of the National Archives, UK.
72	Letter from Radiobats to Companies Registration Office.	Source: National Archives file BT 31/28755/201204 Files of Dissolved Companies: Radiobats Ltd. c. 1924. Reproduced with the kind permission of the National Archives, UK.
73	Letter from General Radio Company Ltd. to Companies Registration Office.	Source: National Archives file BT 31/28755/201204 Files of Dissolved Companies: Radiobats Ltd. c. 1924. Reproduced with the kind permission of the National Archives, UK.
75	Extracts from patent GB180120.	Reproduced with the kind permission of the European Patents Office (EPO) whose website may be found at: http://www.epo.org/index.html Use of content from the EPO website is governed by Article 5 'Copyright, use of content' of the EPO Terms and Conditions which may be found at: http://www.epo.org/footer/terms.html#Copyright
76	Photograph of Mullard P.M.0 valve.	Photo courtesy of Keith Thrower.
79	G.R.C. Radiophones.	Photograph by Ian Sanders.
80	Photograph of General Radio headphones box.	Photo courtesy of Chris Simmonds.
84	G.R.C. Ampliphone loudspeaker.	From the Martyn Bennett collection. Photograph by Lorne Clark.
87	G.R.C.29 Hearthside loudspeaker.	From the Martyn Bennett collection. Photograph by Lorne Clark.
88	G.R.C.28 Pleasure Time loudspeaker.	From the Martyn Bennett collection. Photograph by Lorne Clark.
94	G.R.C.6 dial.	Photograph by Ian Sanders.
96	G.R.C.71 Variometer with embossed General.	Photograph by Ian Sanders.
97	G.R.C.72 Variocoupler, box and accessories envelope.	Photographs by Lorne Clark.
108	G.R.C. B.B.C. label with P.O. Reg. No. 142.	Photograph by Ian Sanders.

Page	Image details	Source and Acknowledgment
108	Original entry showing General Radio Company had subscribed to ten shares in the first BBC return dated 16 March, 1923.	Source: National Archives file BT 31/27633/186424. Reproduced with the kind permission of the National Archives, UK.
109	Original proof of an early version of the Post Office registration conditions, dated October 1922.	© Royal Mail Group Ltd., courtesy of The British Postal Museum & Archive.
112	Three images of a Cox-Cavendish electric shock apparatus.	Photographs courtesy of Gianfranco Rocchini.
113	(Left) Electrical shock machine and label by Cox-Cavendish Electrical Co. Ltd.	Photographs by Ian Sanders.
113	(Right) 'Eros Faradic Battery' and accessorie by Cox-Cavendish Electrical Co. Ltd.	Photographs by Carl Glover.
114	Top three images of a 1922 BTH portable set designed by Reginald Charles Clinker and manufactured by Cox-Cavendish Electrical Co.	Photographs courtesy of John Wakely.
114	Bottom, image of label plate from set, ser. no. R112, held in Science Museum reserve collection store, London.	Photograph by Lorne Clark.
115	Image of BTH sales leaflet for their 1922 portable set.	From the Mike Prince collection. Mike's father, H. Stanley Prince, was retailing wireless sets even before the start of broadcasting in the UK, including this BTH portable set. Our thanks to Mike for allowing us to scan this rare leaflet.
116	Extract from the 12th Report of the Directors of the Cox-Cavendish Electrical Company, dated June 30 1923.	Source: National Archives file BT31/20076/16324 Files of Dissolved Companies: Cox-Cavendish Electrical Co. Ltd. c. 1923. Reproduced with the kind permission of the National Archives, UK.
120	Extract from patent GB241729 showing the structure of the double-fluid cell.	Reproduced with the kind permission of the European Patents Office (EPO) whose website may be found at: http://www.epo.org/index.html Use of content from the EPO website is governed by Article 5 'Copyright, use of content' of the EPO Terms and Conditions which may be found at: http://www.epo.org/footer/terms.html#Copyright
121	Extract from Darimont's patent GB263081.	Reproduced with the kind permission of the European Patents Office (EPO) whose website may be found at: http://www.epo.org/index.html Use of content from the EPO website is governed by Article 5 'Copyright, use of content' of the EPO Terms and Conditions which may be found at: http://www.epo.org/footer/terms.html#Copyright

NEW GENERAL RADIO SET CREATES SENSATION

Loud Speaker & all accessories built into one beautiful cabinet

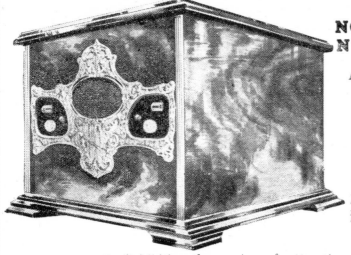

NO ACCUMULATOR: NEW TYPE VALVES

Many other exclusive features

This is the new General Radio Set with its handsome cabinet of genuine hand-polished English walnut, the set is neat, compact, and easily transportable

A T the Radio Exhibition the centre of attraction was the New General Radio Set. This wonderful receiver had so many unique features that everyone was drawn to the General Radio Stand.

NO MORE ACCUMULATORS TO CHARGE! One of the most attractive features of this new set is the absence of the Accumulator. No longer will owners of General Radio Sets need to bother about having accumulators recharged. The General Radio *FILONATOR* (exclusive to General Radio Sets) can be recharged instantly in your own home simply by inserting special compressed tablets costing 1/-, a charge lasting six weeks with average use. It is much more reliable and efficient than the old style accumulator and lasts much longer. There is no acid in the Filonator, no fumes and no danger.

A TRULY REMARKABLE LOUD-SPEAKER Another feature of this new receiver is the patent "Magnetic-Cone" Loud Speaker. Although measuring only six inches across it gives remarkable volume with an exceptional sweetness of tone and a fidelity of reproduction so outstanding that the music or singing could be in the room beside you. The old horn type of speaker has been done away with and this new loud speaker is built into the cabinet. This big step forward is to a great extent responsible for the very handsome appearance of the new General Radio Cabinet Set.

UNUSUALLY EASY TUNING Tuning-in on the new General Radio Set has been made so easy by the new patent "Astatic" vario-coupler that only one control is

needed, this tuning gives so fine an adjustment that you can get the station you want at maximum strength without the slightest trouble. The tuning of the set covers all the European stations *without* additional coils.

SUPER QUALITY VALVES The new General Radio Set is fitted with special new type 1.4 volt valves designed specially by the leading Valve Manufacturers to give maximum efficiency with the General Radio Filonator. They have two filaments so that should one eventually burn out they continue to work on the second filament. This ensures *double life* for each valve.

NO INCREASE IN PRICES

The set complete costs only £12. The royalty is paid and there is *nothing* else to buy. If desired, easy payment terms of 20/- a month for twelve months are available. In every case, and which ever way you buy, all General Radio Sets are

INSTALLED FREE

in your home by our own engineer, in any part of the country. The Set is left playing perfectly for you, and free service calls are given after installation. Never before has so remarkable a set been offered to the public at so low a price and with so much service.

SEND TO-DAY FOR FULL PARTICULARS

Say Catalogue 4C—on a postcard with your name and address—or cut out this advt., write your name and address in the margin and put in open envelope (½d. stamp)

GENERAL RADIO ★

GENERAL RADIO CO., LTD., 235 REGENT STREET, LONDON, W.1   SHOWROOMS: 105 REGENT STREET, LONDON, W.1

The Wireless World and Radio Review, October 12, 1927.

Index

"A Man Called Inventor:
L'intrépide William S. Stephenson."

Canadian postage stamp issued in 1999.

About the Authors

Ian L. Sanders grew up in Harrow, North-West London. His interest in vintage wireless dates from the early 1970s when a student at Cardiff University, Wales where he received B.Eng and Ph.D degrees. Moving to the US in 1977, he has made his home in Northern California's Silicon Valley since 1979. With over thirty years of engineering management experience, he has held several executive positions in the computer data storage industry.

He is the author of numerous articles on various aspects of vintage wireless published on both sides of the Atlantic. In 2006, he was the recipient of the British Vintage Wireless Society's Duncan Neale Award in recognition of his series of books on domestic British crystal sets of the 1920s – Tickling the Crystal.

Ian is a member of the British Vintage Wireless Society. He lives with his wife and daughter in Morgan Hill, California where he has recently published a book of local history.

Lorne Clark was born in Watford, North London. His interest in wireless and 'all things electrical' goes back to his childhood when, at the age of ten, he built his first crystal set disguised as a fountain pen!

After serving an apprenticeship at Marconi Instruments in St. Albans he went on to gain a B.Sc. in Physical Electronics from Newcastle-Upon-Tyne Polytechnic, now part of the University of Northumberland. He joined Racal Instruments as a graduate in 1974, retiring in 2007 as Chief Technical Consultant. As well as giving talks on various radio and broadcasting related topics, Lorne has authored several articles for the Bulletin of the British Vintage Wireless Society and is the author of Shareholders of The British Broadcasting Company published by BVWS Books. He is passionate about preserving the history of broadcasting in the UK, enjoys carrying out research in this field from diverse resources and is Archivist to the British Vintage Wireless Society.

Lorne now lives in Berkshire, UK, with his wife, daughter and son. He is a member of the British Vintage Wireless Society and holds a full UK amateur radio licence.